D1588451

# 1001
# WRISTWATCHES

## HISTORY • TECHNOLOGY • DESIGN

This edition published by Parragon Publishing
Parragon Books Ltd
Queen Street House
4 Queen Street
Bath BA1 1HE, UK

Copyright © 2006 Heel Verlag GmbH, Königswinter
HEEL Verlag GmbH
Gut Pottscheidt
53639 Königswinter
Email: info@heel-verlag.de

Written by: Martin Häussermann
Additional text by: Peter Braun, Gerhard Claussen
Photographs: from the archives of the author and manufacturers
Layout: Grafikbüro Schumacher, Königswinter
Lithography: Colibri, Petra Hammermann, Königswinter

Copyright © 2007 for the UK edition
Parragon Books Ltd
Queen Street House
4 Queen Street
Bath BA1 1HE, UK

UK edition produced by Cambridge Publishing Management Ltd
Translation: Susan James & Theresa Pike
Editing: Juliet Mozley
Proofreading: Alison Rasch

All rights reserved. This publication or any part thereof may not
be reproduced, stored in a retrieval system, or transmitted, in any
form or by any means, electronic, mechanical, photocopying,
recording, or otherwise, without the prior written permission of
the copyright holder.

ISBN 978-1-4075-5272-9

Printed in China

# 1001
# WRISTWATCHES

## HISTORY • TECHNOLOGY • DESIGN

*Martin Häussermann*

Bath · New York · Singapore · Hong Kong · Cologne · Delhi · Melbourne

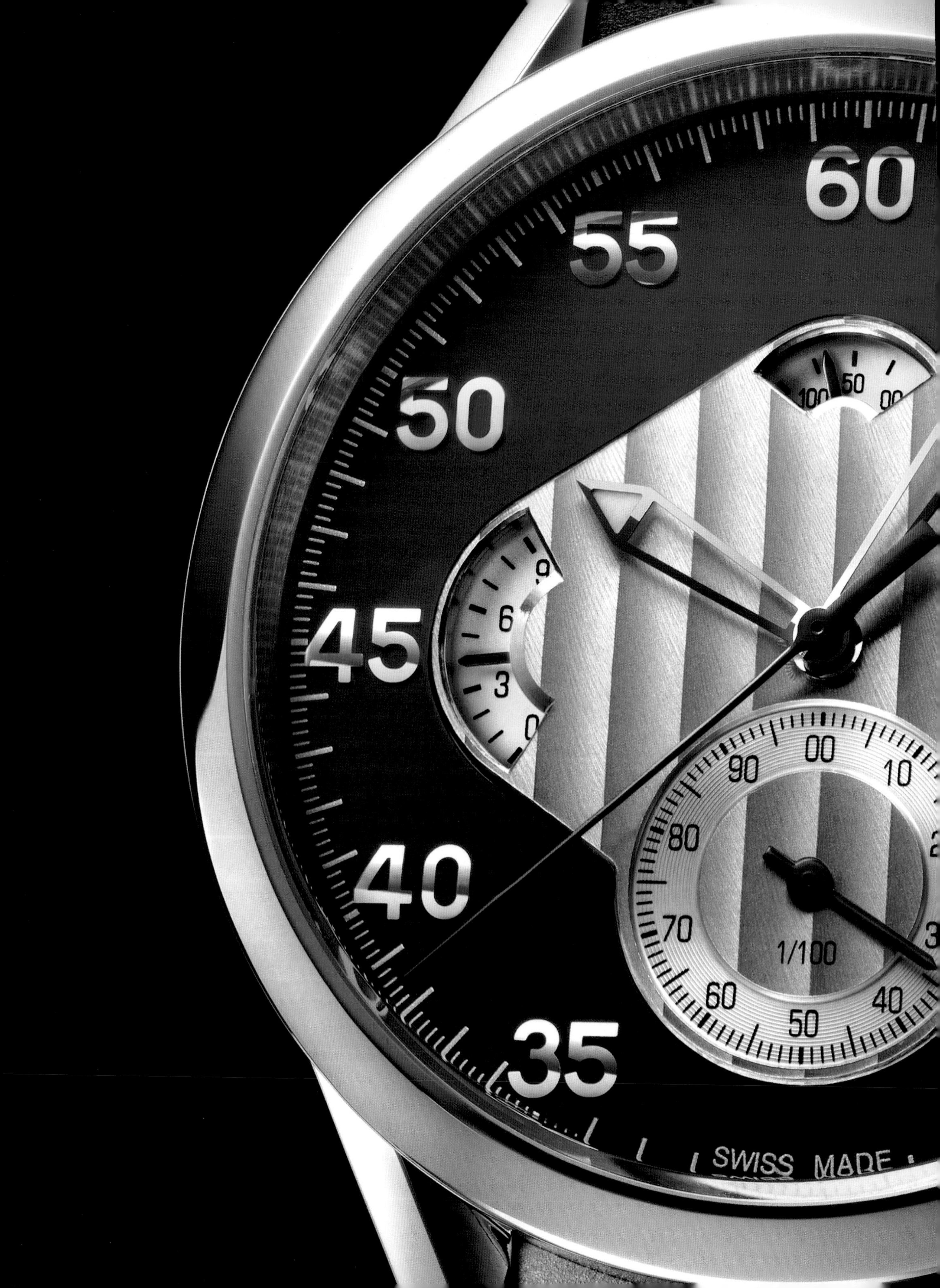

SWISS MADE
1/100

# CONTENTS

# Dear Reader,

To be honest, the mechanical watch is really an anachronism, because a battery-operated quartz watch costing ten pounds is certainly at least as accurate a timepiece. Apart from that there are time displays on mobile phones, organizers, cars, and in aeroplane cockpits. But the fact remains: we wouldn't like to be without our mechanical watches – even in these modern times, or maybe even as an antidote to the digital overkill that poses a daily threat in the workplace and in our everyday life. The mechanical watch invites us to view it not just as a tool, but as a work of art, and to pause a little whilst we do so. It is an expression of personal style, a reliable travelling companion, and thanks to automatic or hand winding, it still tells us the time when the batteries in a quartz watch or mobile phone are fading fast. And that's something they have a tendency to do without warning and at the most inconvenient time.

Another point: at a time when sustainability is the buzzword everywhere you go, what better example can there be than the mechanical watch? It is an investment for life – and even beyond. While batteries and – sooner or later – the whole quartz watch will end up on the rubbish tip, mechanical watches will – sooner or later – simply be passed on. Forgetting all the factual arguments that men in particular need to be able to justify unnecessary purchases such as fast cars, amazing aeroplanes or even expensive watches, we would just like to say: all these things are simply tremendous fun.

At the same time, we're always spoiled for choice, even where watches are concerned. Those of us who are more practically minded choose an automatic watch with an easily read display, which might show the date as well as the time. Those of a more frivolous nature aspire to a chronograph with a stopwatch function that isn't just handy for timing sporting events, but also comes into its own when grilling a steak or boiling an egg. Divers buy special diving watches; pilots and would-be pilots are more likely to favour an aviator watch. Finally, globetrotters opt for a watch that displays different time zones.

This book is a compendium of all sorts of watches arranged according to their purpose and function − with over 1,000 photographs of watches documenting almost 100 years of watch history. It also contains information about the various types of watches and their backgrounds. By the time you've read it, you won't just know the history of the tourbillon, but will also be able to tell the difference between a chronograph and a chronometer.

A propos chronometers, a mechanical watch really is pretty accurate. Good watches, which have been individually adjusted for the wearer, go fast or slow by a maximum of five seconds a day. This equates to an accuracy of 99.9998 per cent.

The editor would sincerely like to thank the authors and photographers who have not just contributed to the success of this book, but who through their regular contributions to the *Armbanduhren* ('Wristwatches') magazine have demonstrated that their technical knowledge of watches is indeed moving with the times.

*Martin Häussermann*

# 1. MEN'S WATCHES

The clock is the oldest independently working mechanical device that we know. The possibility of being able to measure something as vague as time is part of its fascination. This is enhanced by the fact that the mechanical clock is one of the most accurate machines that there is. On the following pages, which are illustrated with the finest men's watches from the past nine decades, we would like to introduce you to the function of a mechanical watch.

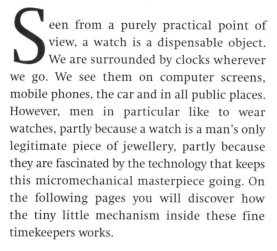

Seen from a purely practical point of view, a watch is a dispensable object. We are surrounded by clocks wherever we go. We see them on computer screens, mobile phones, the car and in all public places. However, men in particular like to wear watches, partly because a watch is a man's only legitimate piece of jewellery, partly because they are fascinated by the technology that keeps this micromechanical masterpiece going. On the following pages you will discover how the tiny little mechanism inside these fine timekeepers works.

Roughly speaking, the movement can be divided into the mainspring, gear train, escapement and regulating system. This arrangement does, however, exclude two vital assemblies, namely the motion work that is required to transform the continuing motion of a movement with

**Audemars Piguet**
Chronometer, yellow gold, manually wound, calibre VZSS, from 1951

**Audemars Piguet**
Ultra-thin, platinum, manually wound, AP calibre 2003, from 1999

**Audemars Piguet**
Men's watch for Cartier, yellow gold, manually wound, calibre 2001LEC, from 1955

**Audemars Piguet**
Jump Hour, white gold, manually wound, from 1925

hands and dial into a practical visual display, and the winding mechanism.

## Winding

'When I wind up my watch should I turn the little wheel in both directions or just in one?' This is a question frequently asked of watchmakers by people who wear a mechanical watch with a manual winding mechanism. It is generally too complicated to explain the technicalities, so he or she might simply reply that when you wind a watch it doesn't matter whether you turn the 'little wheel' (the crown) backwards and forwards between your thumb and index finger, or rotate it forward, reposition your fingers, then rotate forward again. It really doesn't matter, because a watch can only be wound up in one direction,

**Audemars Piguet**
Millenary Automatic, yellow gold, automatic, AP calibre 2125, from 1999

**Audemars Piguet**
Men's watch with digital display, white gold, manually wound, calibre GHSM, from 1929

**Audemars Piguet**
Jules Audemars 3120 'Globe', red gold, automatic, AP calibre 3120, from 2006

**Audemars Piguet**
Automatic, white gold, automatic, calibre K2072, from 1965

**Audemars Piguet**
Royal Oak 'Jumbo', steel, automatic, AP calibre 2121, from 2006

**Audemars Piguet**

Edward Piguet Automatic, red gold, automatic, AP calibre 2121, from 2006

Officine Panerai hand-wind movement with eight-day power reserve

**Baume & Mercier**

Hampton, steel, automatic, Baume & Mercier calibre BM 13750 (base calibre ETA 2000), from 1999

generally by turning the crown clockwise (if you are looking straight at the centre of the crown).

If you turn the crown anticlockwise, you barely feel any resistance, because this is a neutral gear mode. What happens is that the winding pinion and clutch wheel, both of which have identical interlocking ramped teeth, disengage and slide along past each other. This takes us neatly on to the gearing mechanism.

The link between the movement and the outside world is via a thin steel shaft with a long pin at one end, with which it is mounted into a recess in the base plate of the watch. On the other end, which protrudes from the watch, it has a male thread on to which the winding crown is screwed. The term 'winding

stem', generally used for the shaft described here, is actually an inadequate description because it is also used for setting the time, i.e. moving the hands. On modern wristwatches this shaft serves a third function in addition to those of winding and setting the time: it is also used for quick adjustment of the date.

### The power source

The power source of a clockwork movement has remained essentially unchanged for hundreds of years: a long, flat metal spring, coiled up and fixed at both ends. The resulting opposing forces provide the driving power for the watch. When the first pocket watches were invented, the time came to say goodbye to the perfect power source for a clockwork movement: the pendulum. The advantages of the portable clock were somewhat counteracted

**Blancpain**
Villeret ultra-slim, steel, automatic,
Blancpain calibre 1153, from 2006

**Baume & Mercier**
Classima, yellow gold, automatic,
Baume & Mercier calibre BM
18922 (base calibre ETA 2892-
A2), from 1999

**Baume & Mercier**
Hampton Classic, yellow gold, quartz,
ETA 901.001, from 2006

**Blancpain**
Ultra-slim watch, yellow gold,
automatic, Blancpain calibre
1735, from 1999

**Blu**
Terzett, rose gold, automatic, calibre
blu-Orbit (base calibre ETA 2892-A2),
from 2006

**Baume & Mercier**
Classima Executives XL, steel, manually wound,
BM calibre 16498 (base calibre ETA 6498-2), from 2006

**Rainer Brand**
Panama, steel, automatic, ETA calibre
2892-A2, from 1999

**Breguet**
Manually wound, yellow gold, Breguet
calibre 530, from 1999

**Martin Braun**
Bigdate, steel, automatic,
TT calibre 651 (base calibre
ETA 2892-A2), from 2006

by the distinct disadvantage of an irregular power source. A grandfather clock or wall clock with a pendulum is driven by a steady, constant torque. A clock's accuracy is dependent solely upon making adjustments to the gear train, escapement and regulating system (balance/pendulum). Not so, however, with a spring-powered watch. In this case one of the possible causes for timekeeping errors lies in the uncoiling action of the mainspring, as the power curve is non-linear.

## The spring

The mainspring provides the energy that drives the watch. A spring-powered movement is the only mechanism that requires just one burst of energy to provide its services for up to 45 hours (and in the case of modern automatic watches, for far in excess of 50 hours) without the addition of fuel, air pressure or steam. A turbine cannot function without a continuous supply of steam, nor can a car engine run without fuel burning constantly, and the modern household collapses if deprived of electricity. The quartz watch and the car

**Bulova**
Limited Edition, yellow gold,
automatic ETA calibre 1120,
from 1999

**Breguet**
Tonneau, yellow gold,
automatic, Breguet calibre
532, from 1999

**Bunz**
Moontime, steel/yellow gold,
automatic, ETA calibre 2892-2,
from 1999

**Breguet**
Classic ultra-slim, yellow gold,
automatic, Breguet calibre 502.3,
from 2006

**Bvlgari**
Bvlgari, platinum, automatic, Bvlgari
calibre BU220 (base calibre Girard-
Perregaux 220), from 2006

25

**Bvlgari**
Bvlgari Moon Phases, white gold,
automatic, LIP calibre 3103 (base
calibre ETA 2892-A2), from 2006

**Cartier**
Crash watch, yellow gold, manually
wound, from 1991

**Cartier**
Square, yellow gold, manually
wound, from 1970

**Cartier**
Santos Dumont, manually wound,
calibre 21, from 1980

have one thing in common: if the tank (coin cell) is empty, the only thing they are both still capable of doing is showing us the extent to which we depend upon them. The question as to whether a mainspring is, figuratively speaking, a fuel or an engine isn't that easy to answer – it's both.

The mainspring isn't like a rubber band, which can be stretched, but when released relaxes and finally hangs slack. Even the spring of a watch that has run down still has a considerable residual tension and would continue to uncoil quite a lot if there was sufficient room within the watch. Mainsprings are literally as hard as steel, have a very dense molecular structure and are accordingly brittle. In days gone by, when springs made from cold rolled steel were used, the task of replacing a mainspring that had

suddenly snapped for no particular reason was a regular job for any watchmaker.

'I've overwound my watch', confesses the guilty customer to the watchmaker. But just to clear up a widespread misunderstanding: even the owner of a delicate ladies' watch would have to take a pair of pliers to her little watch to 'overwind' the mainspring. This holds true today more than ever, because in normal use the springs used in modern watches are unbreakable. As usual, the exception proves the rule. The replacement mainsprings used so frequently by watchmakers in the past were either simple flat-rolled steel bands that had acquired their material springiness through hardening and tempering, or their residual stress by cold rolling. These springs had a hole at each end. One hole was used to attach one

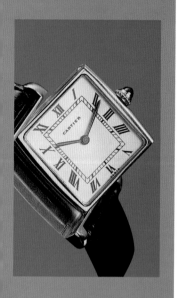

**Cartier**
Reverso, yellow gold, manually
wound, calibre 838/1, from 1980

**Cartier**
Santos 100, red gold, automatic, Cartier calibre 49 (base calibre
ETA 2892), from 2006

**Cartier**
Roadster XL, steel, automatic, Cartier calibre 8500 (base calibre
ETA 2893), from 2006

**Cartier**
Pasha de Cartier, white gold,
automatic, Cartier calibre 115,
24-hour display, from 1999

end of the spring to the hook on what is known
as the barrel arbour. The other end was secured
to the hook of the barrel within which the
spring was now coiled.

When the winding stem of the watch is turned
and this turning action is transferred to the
ratchet wheel via the clutch wheel, winding
pinion and crown wheel, the transfer of power
to the movement also begins. At this moment
the mainspring, which up until now had been
wound hard up against the wall of the barrel,
and which is attached by its hole to a hook on
the barrel arbour, is drawn to the centre of the
barrel. With every turn of the winding crown,
the mainspring winds itself tighter around the
barrel arbour. At the same time it tries to pull
the barrel itself along with it, in an attempt
to uncoil itself again as far as possible. In
consequence the barrel begins to turn, and its
toothed rim transmits the driving force to the
watch's gear train.

## The driving force

### Modern springs
The development of the springs used nowadays
goes back to the Swiss engineer Max Straumann,
who at the beginning of the fifties introduced
a new development in the area of watch
springs under the name of 'Nivaflex'. In
numerous experiments Straumann had made
up an alloy from iron, nickel, chrome, cobalt,
beryllium and other additives. Springs
manufactured from this material are rust-
resistant, unbreakable, cannot be magnetized
and are fatigue-proof. A Nivaflex spring can
be wound up 10,000 times without losing its
strength, so if wound up daily, it will give more
than 27 years' reliable service. The springs
used today are coated with a special lubricating
layer, which means that they don't require
further lubrication by a watchmaker and
ensures reduced friction between the individual
layers of the spring.

**Chopard**
Tonneau Power Reserve, yellow gold, automatic, Frédéric Piguet calibre 9644, power reserve indicator, from 1999

**Chopard**
L.U.C. 1.96, yellow gold, automatic, L.U.C. calibre 1.96, C.O.S.C. certified chronometer, from 2006

**Chronoswiss**
Régulateur Réctangulaire, yellow gold, manually wound, calibre FHF 29 (introduced 1934), from 1993

**Chopard**
St. Moritz, steel, automatic, Jaeger-LeCoultre calibre 889, from 1999

**Chopard**
L.U.C. Quattro, platinum, manually wound, L.U.C. calibre 1.98, C.O.S.C. certified chronometer, from 2006

**Chronoswiss**
Régulateur, steel, automatic, Chronoswiss calibre C.122 (base calibre Enicar 165), from 1999

**Chronoswiss**
Kairos, steel, automatic, base calibre
ETA 2892-2, from 1999

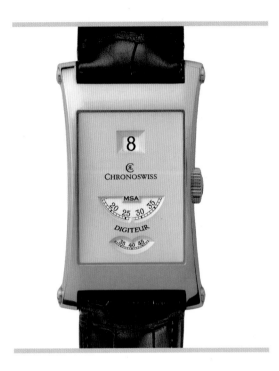

**Chronoswiss**
Digiteur, red gold, automatic,
FEF calibre 130, from 2006

### The gear train

In a mechanical watch the parts of the gear train are akin to an industrial labourer whose performance within the system as a whole is rarely mentioned, but who is nevertheless an important and indispensable member of the team. It is rare for the 'workers' in the 'gear train department' of a watch to put in an official appearance. The balance and anchor, the hands and dial are always in the limelight. But who knows what a third wheel or fourth wheel pinion is? These unsung workers, who make sure that the power from the mainspring arrives, much changed, at the regulating system, deserve a special mention. 'It's running like clockwork', is a phrase we sometimes say when we want to emphasize that something is going particularly well. A precision-made and perfectly functioning gear train is a prerequisite

**Chronoswiss**
Orea, steel, manually wound,
Chronoswiss calibre C.111, from 1999

**Chronoswiss**
Régulateur, yellow gold, automatic,
Chronoswiss calibre C.122 (base
calibre Enicar 165), from 2006

for accurate timekeeping. For watchmakers the 'train' is always primarily the toothed gearing that starts at the gear rim of the barrel and ends at the escapement wheel pinion.

## Two operating systems

### Enigmatic workers with unusual names

To the layman the names of the wheels appear somewhat confusing. For instance, the minute wheel doesn't carry the minute hand, nor does it make one revolution in one minute. It is the second wheel that carries the cannon pinion, which bears the minute hand, and it makes one revolution in one hour. And it is the fourth wheel, which carries the seconds hand on its extended pinion, that makes one revolution in one minute.

If we take the minute and fourth wheels as an example, it is clear that the watch designer doesn't have a great deal of room for manoeuvre when designing a watch movement. He has to configure it in such a way that the minute wheel and its pinion go round once in one hour, whilst the fourth wheel must make 60 revolutions within that same time-span. The speed with which the other wheels of the movement turn, the number of teeth on the wheels and pinions, the length and strength of the mainspring, or the number of vibrations per hour of the balance – all of these issues are irrelevant for a watch's time display as long as the gear ratios are configured in such a way that the minute wheel and fourth wheel make the requisite number of revolutions.

**Corum**
Admiral's Cup, steel, quartz driven,
ETA calibre 256.111, from 1999

**Cimier**
C1951 Automatic, steel, automatic,
ETA calibre 2836-2, from 2006

**Frédérique Constant**
Classic Heartbeat Manufacture Moon, steel,
manually wound, Frédérique Constant calibre
FC 915, with moon phase display, from 2006

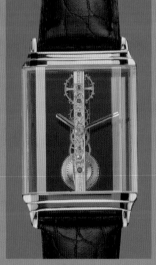

**Corum**
Golden Bridge, yellow gold, manually
wound, Corum calibre Golden Bridge,
from 1999

Elegant men's watches in gold-plated steel casing from Edox, Cimier and Davosa.

**Corum**
US$20 Coin Watch, yellow gold, automatic, Corum calibre CO 082 (base calibre ETA 2892-A2), from 2006

**Cuervo y Sobrinos**
Prominente S.T., steel, automatic, ETA calibre 2671, from 2006

**Cyclos**
a.m./p.m., steel, automatic, Cyclos calibre CW 1 (base calibre ETA 2992-A2), C.O.S.C. certified chronometer, extending and retracting hour hand, from 2006

**Corum**
Bubble Skeleton, steel, automatic, ETA calibre 2892-A2, full skeleton dial, from 2006

The hour wheel, which carries the hour hand known to many as the 'little' hand, makes its revolution once every 12 hours. However, the hour wheel belongs not to the gear train, but to the motion works. These design features only become important when the watchmaker is considering the length of time a watch is required to run after a single winding, or the type of escapement or regulating system that is going to be used. As a minute wheel goes round only approximately once every hour, the selection and interaction of the other parts of the movement are crucial in the watchmaker's quest to achieve perfection, whereby the minute wheel must make one revolution in exactly one hour, and by the end of that hour the second hand must have made its tiny, jerky movements around the dial exactly 60 times. A fully wound wristwatch would unwind in less than a minute if it wasn't stopped in its

**Davosa**
Classic, steel, manually wound, ETA calibre 2804, from 2006

### De Grisogono
Instrumento No.Uno., steel, automatic, ETA 2892-A2 with module for dual time zone display, from 2006

### Du Bois & Fils
Montre Classique, yellow gold, automatic, ETA calibre 2892-A2, from 2006

### Delma
Le Brassus, steel, automatic, ETA calibre 2892-A2, from 1999

### Dubey & Schaldenbrand
Aerodyn Chronometer, steel, automatic, ETA calibre 2892-A2 with 24-hour display, from 1999

### Delma
Klondike 1998, yellow gold, automatic, ETA calibre 2892-A2, power reserve indicator and 24-hour display, from 1999

**Dubey & Schaldenbrand**
Aerodyn Trophée, rose gold, Aurore calibre 19, from 2006

**Ebel**
1911, steel, quartz driven, Ebel calibre 187, from 1999

**Eberhard**
Aqua 8, steel, manually wound, base calibre ETA 7001 Peseux with module for eight-day power reserve, from 1999

**Enigma**
Bezel Manual Winder, steel, manually wound, ETA calibre Peseux 7001, power reserve display, winding and adjustment of hands by rotating bezel, from 1999

**Louis Erard**
Longue Ligne Power Reserve, steel, manually wound, ETA calibre Peseux 7001, power reserve display, from 1999

**Eterna**
KonTiki 20, steel, automatic, Eterna calibre 1489K, from 1968

**Louis Erard**
Heritage Cadran Paris, steel, automatic, ETA calibre 2824-2, from 2006

**Eterna**
1935, steel, automatic, ETA calibre 2681, from 1999

**Eberhard**
Les Grandes Courbées, steel, automatic, Eberhard calibre 3513 (base calibre ETA 2892-A2), power reserve display, from 2006

tracks by the escapement and balance wheel. The only visible sign of its work is the jerky way in which the second hand makes its revolutions.

## The imperfect drive

Each gear drive is basically a testament to the theoretical possibilities of what can be achieved in practice. One might think that two circular discs that glide smoothly over each other would form the ideal basis for a perfect gear train. Unfortunately, however, the theory of the perfect gear train does not take into account the practical issues, for example, wear and tear of the surfaces interacting with each other, slippage (i.e. the sliding of the discs upon one another), improper storage, imbalances and a whole variety of other factors.

**Eterna**
Porsche Design P 10, steel, automatic, Eterna Matic calibre 633 (base calibre ETA 2824-2), from 1999

**Eterna**
1948 Grand Date, steel, automatic,
Eterna calibre 608 (base calibre
ETA 2892-A2) from 2006

**Fabergé**
Agathon, white gold, automatic,
ETA calibre 2892-A2, from 2006

**Gérald Genta**
Retro Les Fantasies, steel, automatic,
Gérald Genta calibre GA3 (base calibre
ETA 2892-A2), from 1999

**Jacques Etoile**
Lune & Etoile, steel, automatic,
ETA calibre 2824-2 with moon
phase display, from 2006

It was for this reason that mechanical engineers and watch designers both chose to go down the route of the second best, but more practically realistic option: a toothed system. Whilst in mechanical engineering gear wheels with triangular teeth with flattened points are generally used, in watch manufacture, what is called a (pseudo) cycloid gear mechanism is used.

In this kind of tooth system the sides of the teeth have a curved, almost half-rounded profile, enabling them to 'roll off' each other easily. This reduces the energy-sapping friction between the wheels. Two wheels in a watch movement rarely engage with each other – a wheel engages with not another wheel, but a pinion. In watchmaking language the pinion is a cogwheel with fewer than 15 teeth. A pinion is generally made from polished, hardened steel, whilst the gear wheels are brass (and very rarely from beryllium bronze).

The barrel of a fully wound spring in a wall clock cannot be brought to a standstill with one's bare hands, but the escape wheel of the same clock can be stopped with a light touch of the finger: 'Gear trains convert high torque with a low rotational speed into low torque with a high rotational speed'. This example clearly shows how great the loss of power is in a clockwork movement, and how small a force is required to drive the tiny movement within a ladies' watch.

## Lots of power for just a short time

A movement without an escapement differs in how it works only marginally from the old spring-driven toys that used to be notorious for having to be wound up every couple of minutes, and that now fetch a high price at auction because of their rarity value.

As there are no gear ratios of 1:1 in the movement (apart from indirectly in the motion work), the speed of rotation changes every time that the gears mesh. At the same time the torque reduces. Compared with the power that

**Girard-Perregaux**
Ferrari President, steel, automatic,
Girard-Perregaux calibre 2200,
from 1999

**Gérald Genta**
Backtimer, white gold, automatic, base calibre Jaeger-LeCoultre
899 with three-digit countdown day timer, from 1999

**Girard-Perregaux**
Vintage 1945, steel, rose gold, automatic, Girard-Perregaux
calibre 3000, from 1999

**Paul Gerber**
Model 33 Moon Phase, rose gold, manual wind, Gerber calibre 33
with moon phase display, from 2006

**Paul Gerber**
Retro Twin, yellow gold, automatic Gerber calibre 15 (base calibre
ETA 7001), retrograde seconds hand, from 2006

**Glashütter
Uhrenbetrieb GUB**
Men's watch 01, yellow gold, manual
wind, GUB calibre 28, from 1950

**Glashütte Original**
Julius Assmann 2, rose gold, manual wind, Glashütte Original calibre 52, watch face from Meissen porcelain, from 1999

**Glashütter Uhrenbetrieb GUB**
Spezimatic, yellow gold, automatic, GUB calibre 661, from 1955

**Glashütte Original**
Senator Automatic Panorama Date, rose gold, automatic, Glashütte Original calibre 39-41, from 1999

**Glashütte Original**
Karree Small Seconds, rose gold, manual wind, Glashütte Original calibre 42-05, from 1999

**Glashütte Original**
1845 Régulateur, rose gold, manual wind, Glashütte Original calibre 49-04, from 1999

**Glashütte Original**
Senator Automatic, rose gold, automatic, Glashütte Original calibre 39-10, from 1999

arrives at the escape wheel, the torque delivered by the mainspring to the barrel is enormous.

The change in rotational speed between the barrel and the escape wheel is also very great. By the time the ponderous barrel has made just one revolution, the harassed escape wheel has already completed hundreds. It is therefore highly possible for a delicate escape wheel pivot to be simply ripped off by its own speed if the fully wound movement runs unchecked, particularly if the oil film surrounding it is no longer perfect.

Without an escapement, or more precisely without the escape lever, a fully wound movement would run down within a very short time. With a watch this takes less than a minute, while with a clock it can take as much as half an hour. So on the one hand, the escapement checks the uncontrolled, fast running of the train. On the other hand, it transfers the by now greatly reduced power from the mainspring, which has been transmitted through the gear train, to the oscillating system.

## The escapement

The German term for the escapement is *die Hemmung*, which means 'inhibition', and in the same way as the suggestion that a person should 'not have any inhibitions' could lead to dire consequences, the effect of a watch losing its inhibitions – its escapement – would be equally catastrophic. It is the escapement that turns a spring-driven mechanism into a device for measuring time. It is at one and the same time a driver and something that is driven.

The escapement consists of an escape lever and an escape wheel. The escape lever is also known

**Harwood**
Automatic, steel, automatic, ETA calibre 2892-2, winding and adjustment of hands via rotating bezel, from 1999

**Glashütte Original**
PanoReserve, rose gold, manual wind, Glashütte Original calibre 65-01, power reserve display, from 2006

**Glashütte Original**
PanoMaticLunar, steel, automatic, Glashütte Original calibre 90-02, moon phase display, from 2006

**Harwood**
Automatic Louis Reguin, steel, automatic, ETA calibre 2892-2, winding and adjustment of hands via rotating bezel, from 2006

41

**Heuer**
Abercrombie & Fitch Solunar, steel, manual wind, tidal indicator at six o'clock, from 1948

**IWC**
Men's watch, silver, manual wind, from 1918

**Hermès**
Dressage, red gold, automatic, Vaucher calibre P 1928, from 2006

**Hublot**
Elegant, yellow gold, automatic, Frédéric Piguet calibre 9511, from 1999

**IWC**
Yacht Club II, steel, automatic, calibre IWC 3254, from 1976

as an anchor because of its shape, which generally resembles that of a ship's anchor.

Broadly speaking, the main function of the escapement is to check – to 'inhibit' – the rotation of the clockwork wheels. At the same time it is responsible for converting the rotation of the escape wheel into the pendulum motion of the oscillating system (pendulum or balance). Conversely, the oscillating system prevents the escapement from completely stopping the movement, because the pendulum or balance forces the escapement to allow the gear train to rotate, step by step, allowing it to 'escape'.

In English we talk of the 'escapement' and in French the *échappement*, both of which imply 'escaping' or 'getting free'. However the German term *Hemmung* ('inhibition') means the opposite. It is reminiscent of the glass that

## IWC

Engineer SL, yellow gold, automatic, calibre IWC 8541B, protected from magnetic fields by soft iron inner case, from 1973

## IWC

Portuguese, steel, manual wind, calibre IWC 982, from 1975

## IWC

Men's watch, yellow gold, manual wind, calibre IWC8, from 1941

## IWC

Portuguese Automatic, platinum, automatic, IWC calibre 887/2, from 1999

## IWC

Engineer, steel, automatic, calibre IWC 8531, only 250 pieces were manufactured with this watch face, from 1960

### IWC
Engineer Automatic, steel, automatic, IWC calibre 80110, protected from magnetic fields by soft iron inner case, from 2006

### IWC
Portofino Automatic, red gold, IWC calibre 30110 (base calibre ETA 2892-A2), from 2006

### IWC
Portuguese Automatic, white gold, automatic, IWC calibre 50010, eight-day power reserve, from 2006

### Jaeger-LeCoultre
Men's watch with digital display, rose gold, manual wind, JLC calibre 480CW, from 1950

### Jaeger-LeCoultre
Reverso, steel, manual wind, JLC calibre, from 1935

### Jaeger-LeCoultre
Master Ultrathin, red gold, automatic, JLC calibre 849, from 1999

**Jaeger-LeCoultre**
Master Control, red gold, automatic,
JLC calibre 899, from 2006

**Jaeger-LeCoultre**
LeCoultre Futurematic, yellow gold,
automatic, JLC calibre 497, with
bumper automatic movement and
power reserve display, crown on rear
of the casing, from 1940

**Jaeger-LeCoultre**
Reverso Grande Date, steel,
manual wind, JLC calibre 875,
power reserve display, from 2006

**Jaeger-LeCoultre**
Reverso Classique, yellow gold,
manual wind, JLC calibre 846,
from 1999

**Jaeger-LeCoultre**
Reverso Grande Taille, yellow gold,
manual wind, JLC calibre 822, from
1999

45

**Daniel JeanRichard**
TV Screen Automatic, steel, automatic, JR calibre 24DJR (base calibre ETA 2824-2), from 1999

**JeanRichard**
Grand TV Screen Double Retrograde, rose gold, automatic, JR calibre 23 (base calibre ETA 2892-A2), retrograde date and seconds display, from 2006

**Junghans**
Chronometer, high-grade steel, manual wind, Junghans calibre 62.1, from 1960

**Junghans**
Max Bill, steel, manual wind, ETA calibre 2801-2, from 1999

**Kelek**
Automatic with power reserve, steel, automatic, Kelek calibre 7000 (base calibre ETA 2892-A2), power reserve display, from 1999

**Kurth**
Skeleton watch, rose gold, manual wind, historic ETA calibre from the 1940s, from 1999

**A. Lange & Söhne**
Men's watch, yellow gold, manual wind, Lange calibre 10 ½", from 1944

**Maurice Lacroix**
Jumping hour, steel/yellow gold, manual wind, calibre ML 28 (base calibre Peseux 7046), from 1999

**Maurice Lacroix**
Tiago skeleton watch, steel, automatic, calibre ML14 (base calibre ETA 2892-2), from 1999

**Maurice Lacroix**
Pontos Réserve de Marche, steel, automatic, ETA calibre 2897, power reserve display, from 2006

is half-full or half-empty, depending upon whether one is an optimist or a pessimist – identical contents, but different points of view. The German clock is inhibited or checked; the English or French clock is freed. But, realistically speaking, English and French clocks do also have to be inhibited, and it's only at that point that something is also allowed to run away – namely the gear train.

And despite its 'inhibitions', it still runs at a fast and furious pace. In one hour the escape wheel of a modern mechanical movement completes 28,800 little steps. The pallet is flung backwards and forwards by the unremitting balance exactly the same number of times as the steps, with repeatedly renewed vigour. In comparison with a car engine this is, of course, still a snail's pace. However, if one considers that the barrel barely moves in one hour, the increase in speed is quite considerable.

With the majority of today's escapement mechanisms the all-important braking of the train is accomplished by two 'claws' (pallets) on the anchor, which alternately engage the teeth of the escape wheel, thereby stopping it from turning. The anchor is a lever with two

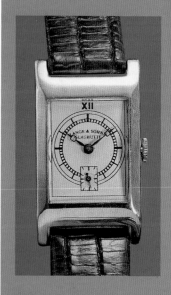

**A. Lange & Söhne**
Men's watch, yellow gold, manual wind, Lange shaped movement, from 1932

**A. Lange & Söhne**
Langematik, white gold, automatic,
Lange calibre L921.2, from 1999

**A. Lange & Söhne**
Lange 1, yellow gold, manual wind,
Lange calibre L901.0, from 1999

**A. Lange & Söhne**
1815 Up and Down, yellow gold, manual
wind, Lange calibre L942.1, from 1999

**A. Lange & Söhne**
Cabaret, yellow gold, manual wind,
Lange calibre L931.3, from 1999

**A. Lange & Söhne**
1815 Automatic, yellow gold, automatic,
Lange calibre L921.2, from 2006

**A. Lange & Söhne**
Saxonia, yellow gold, manual wind,
Lange calibre L941.3, from 2006

**A. Lange & Söhne**
1815, white gold, manual wind,
Lange calibre L941.1, from 2006

**A. Lange & Söhne**
Cabaret, yellow gold, manual
wind, Lange calibre L931.3,
from 2006

**Limes**
Pharo Power Reserve, steel, manual
wind, ETA calibre 7001 with Soprod
power reserve module, from 2006

**A. Lange & Söhne**
Langematik, yellow gold,
automatic, Lange calibre L921.4
SAX-O-MAT, from 2006

**Longines**
Men's watch, steel, manual wind,
Longine calibre 13.34 with enamel
face, from 1915

49

**Longines**

Doctor's Watch, steel, manual wind, Longines calibre 9.32, shaped movement, from 1931

**Longines**

Hour Glass, steel/gold-plated, manual wind, Longines calibre 9.LT, from 1954

**Longines**

Master Collection Automatic, steel, automatic, Longines calibre L619 (base calibre ETA 2892-A2), from 2006

**Longines**

Mystérieuse, white gold, manual wind, Longines calibre 237, hour display via central rotating disc, from 1957

**Jean Marcel**

Mystery Tonneau World Map, steel, automatic, ETA calibre 2824 with Jean Marcel module, revolving face with digital jumping hour, from 1999

**Jean Marcel**

Automatic, steel, automatic, ETA calibre 2688, from 1999

## Braking claws

limbs made from hardened steel (or, in clocks, from brass and steel). The axis of rotation of the anchor lies at the point of intersection of the vertical and horizontal shafts.

The pallets of watch anchors are synthetic rubies that are inset into the steel body of the anchor, and fixed with a tiny drop of shellac, or, more often nowadays, with a special glue.

Driven by spring power or a weight, the escape wheel just wants to turn. So it finds the pallets that keep sticking between its teeth extremely aggravating. There is always an escape tooth in contact with one of the anchor pallets, or more specifically with what is termed the 'locking face' on the edge of the pallet.

As the pendulum swings, the anchor also has to perform the same movement. As it does so, the

**MeisterSinger**
Edition Scrypto 1Z, manual wind, ETA calibre 6497-1, hour display only, from 2006

**Mido**

Commander Chronometer, steel, automatic, ETA calibre 2836-2, from 2006

**Milus**

Xephios, steel, automatic, ETA calibre 2836-2, from 2006

**Minerva**

Pythagore Anniversary, steel, manual wind, Minerva calibre 48, from 1999

point of one of the escape teeth – which is continuously pressing against the pallet – slides from its locking face on the side to the impulse face on the front of the pallet.

At last the escape wheel has the opportunity to move itself slightly. The escape tooth contacts the well-lubricated impulse face of the releasing pallet, giving it an upward push, at the same time pushing the anchor farther away from its original position. The arms of the anchor transfer the impulse via the shaft, at the end of which there is a small fork with a notch. In this way the anchor provides the pendulum with the small amount of momentum needed for it to swing steadily. Then the escape tooth slips off the impulse face of the pallet (an act termed the drop), and on the opposite side of the anchor, another of the escape teeth engages with the locking face of the second pallet and remains at rest until released.

For obvious reasons a pendulum is unsuitable for a portable clock. So the inventor of the pocket watch was confronted with the task of designing a clock that could perform its

**Movado**

Polyplan, white gold, manual wind, Movado calibre 400, from 1930

**Movado**

SE Automatic, steel, automatic, ETA calibre 2892-A2, from 2006

**Movado**
Men's watch, steel, manual wind,
Movado calibre 261, from 1945

**Movado**
Viziomatic, steel,
auto-quartz, ETA calibre
205.911, from 1999

**Movado**
Museum Watch Safiro Limited Edition,
rose gold, manual wind, Frédéric
Piguet calibre 21P, from 1999

**Franck Muller**
Cintrée Curvex Seconde Rétrograde,
white gold, automatic, FM calibre
7500, from 1999

**Movado**
Botelo Automatic, steel,
automatic, ETA calibre 2824-2,
from 2006

## Franck Muller
Cintrée Curvex Jumping Hour, yellow gold, automatic, FM calibre 7500, from 1999

## Franck Muller
Long Island, white gold, automatic, FM calibre 2800, from 2006

## Nouvelle Horologie Calabrese
Analogica, steel, automatic, ETA calibre 2892-A2 modified by Vincent Calabrese, digital hour display with minute index, from 2006

## Nienaber
King Size RetroLator, steel, manual wind, AS calibre 1130, jumping minute hand, jumping hour hand, from 2006

## Omega
Seamaster Railmaster XXL Chronometer, steel, automatic, Omega calibre 2201 (base calibre ETA 6498), C.O.S.C. certified chronometer, from 2006

function in any position, a clock that would still show the time if its wearer was doing a headstand – provided that it didn't fall out of his waistcoat pocket while he was doing so!

The solution to the problem of returning the regulating device to its neutral position without relying exclusively on the force of gravity came a step closer with the invention of the balance spring. We can credit this enormous leap forward in the development of the pocket watch to an ingenious Dutchman, Christiaan Huygens, who in 1675 was the first person to bend a thin, flexible wire into a spiral and use it to operate a regulating device.

The next stage of development on the quest to design a robust, less sensitive precision watch, a variation of which we are still using at the beginning of the twenty-first century, was

**Nomos**
Tangente Date Power Reserve, steel, manual wind, Nomos calibre Delta with power reserve display, from 2006

**Nomos**
Orion, steel, manual wind, ETA calibre Peseux 7001, from 1999

**Nomos**
Tetra, steel, manual wind, Nomos calibre Alpha, from 2006

**Omega**
Seamaster XVI, red gold, automatic, Omega calibre 471, special model for the 16th Olympic Games in Melbourne, from 1956

**Nomos**
Tangente, steel, manual wind, Nomos calibre Alpha, from 2006

**Omega**

Men's watch, yellow gold, manual wind, Omega calibre 302, from 1955

**Omega**

De Ville Tonneau, steel, automatic, Omega calibre 1120 (base calibre ETA 2892-A2), C.O.S.C. certified chronometer, from 1999

**Omega**

Seamaster Automatic Chronometer, yellow gold, automatic, Omega calibre 751, C.O.S.C. certified chronometer, from 1956

**Omega**

Seamaster Omegamatic, steel, uni-directional rotating diving bezel, quartz with automatic wind, Omega calibre 1400 (base calibre ETA 205.111), from 1999

**Oris**

Rectangular Classic, Oris calibre 583 (base calibre 2688/2671), from 1999

**Oris**
Big Crown Pointer Date, steel,
automatic, Oris calibre 654 (base
calibre ETA 2824-2), from 2006

the invention of the 'free anchor' or 'detached lever' escapement by the English watchmaker Thomas Mudge (1715–1794).

The crucial difference between the 'detached' lever escapement and other kinds of escapement is that, in the case of the latter, the pendulum or balance wheel is linked permanently and inseparably to the escapement and is therefore always subject to interference from the movement. This means that although the oscillating system is supplied with power, the permanent link means that at the same time, it is also deprived of power again. The balance wheel in the escapement invented by Mudge has no such problems. After the balance wheel has received the impulse from the anchor, it is completely free – hence the name of 'free' anchor escapement. This is actually a bit ambiguous, because it is not the escapement but the balance wheel that is 'freed'.

**Panerai**
Radiomir base, steel, manual wind,
Panerai calibre OP X, C.O.S.C.
certified chronometer, from 2006

**Officine Panerai**
Luminor Marina, steel, manual wind, ETA calibre
6497-2, C.O.S.C. certified chronometer, from 1999

**Officine Panerai**
Luminor Submersible, titanium,
automatic, ETA calibre 7750, from 1999

**Parmigiani**
Kalpa XL Hebdomadaire, steel,
manual wind, Parmigiani calibre 110,
eight-day power reserve, from 2006

**Parmigiani**
Bugatti 370 Type, steel, manual wind, Parmigiani calibre 370, ten-day power reserve, from 2006

**Péquignet**
Moorea Power Reserve, steel/yellow gold, automatic, ETA calibre 2892-2 with module for power reserve display, from 1999

**Patek Philippe**
Calatrava, yellow gold, manual wind, Patek Philippe calibre 91, from 1953

**Patek Philippe**
Art Deco men's watch, white gold, manual wind, Patek Philippe calibre 10, from 1928

**Patek Philippe**
Men's watch, yellow gold, manual wind, Patek Philippe calibre 10, from 1932

**Patek Philippe**
Asymmétrique, yellow gold, manual wind, Patek Philippe calibre 91, from 1935

**Patek Philippe**
Men's watch for Gübelin, yellow gold, manual wind, Patek Philippe calibre 9-90, from 1951

**Patek Philippe**
Men's watch, white gold, automatic, Patek Philippe calibre 1-350, from 1976

## The oscillating system

With the introduction of the balance wheel, the watchmaker was confronted with all sorts of problems that he had never previously encountered. Whilst the pendulum of a wall clock or grandfather clock always has the same oscillation amplitude (provided that there is an even power supply, e.g. through weight propulsion), and can generally continue its work unimpeded by outside influences (apart from maybe fluctuations in air pressure and temperature), the balance wheel of a wristwatch is subject to a whole range of adversities that can interfere with the accurate running of the watch. It is not gentle, gliding motion that affects the balance wheel, but the persistent short, sharp movements when changing between a sloping position and the vertical or horizontal. The watch and, by default, the balance wheel have to withstand this rough handling in humid tropical climates or icy cold conditions, when diving or when mountain climbing.

**Perrelet**
Dipteros/Temptest, steel, automatic, Perrelet calibre DH95, from 1999

**Patek Philippe**
Moon Phase, yellow gold, automatic, Patek Philippe calibre 240/154, moon phase and power reserve display, from 1999

59

**Patek Philippe**

Calatrava, yellow gold, automatic,
Patek Philippe calibre 240PS,
from 1999

**Patek Philippe**

Gondolo, yellow gold, automatic,
Patek Philippe calibre 315/190,
from 1999

**Patek Philippe**

Neptune, yellow gold,
automatic, Patek Philippe
calibre 315/190, from 1999

**Patek Philippe**

Aquanaut, steel, automatic, Patek
Philippe calibre 330/194, from 1999

**Patek Philippe**

Calatrava Grande Taille, yellow gold,
automatic, Patek Philippe calibre
315SC, from 2006

### Piaget
Tradition, white gold, automatic, Piaget calibre 190P, C.O.S.C. certified chronometer, from 1999

### Patek Philippe
Nautilus, steel, automatic, Patek Philippe calibre 330/194, from 1999

### Patek Philippe
Nautilus, steel, automatic, Patek Philippe calibre 240 PS IRM C LU, moon phase and power reserve display, from 2006

### Patek Philippe
Gondolo, white gold, manual wind, Patek Philippe calibre 215 PS, from 2006

There is no other technical mechanism that is permanently subjected to such unremitting constant stress as the watch. Year in, year out, this test of stamina is endured by these little machines which contain screws so tiny that 10,000 of them would not fill a single thimble. Little machines in which a metal spiral spring coils and uncoils almost 30,000 times (sometimes more) in one hour, a spring that is so thin it makes a hair from a human head look like a rope next to it. Little machines whose turning parts are lubricated with an amount of oil which is barely perceptible even when viewed through a magnifying glass.

If subjected to similar treatment, a car would be ready for the scrap heap within the space of a few hours. We expect absolute precision from a wristwatch for years. A watch running with a rate deviation of ten seconds per day is working with a tolerance of approximately 0.1 per mille!

### Piaget
Légende Rectangle à l'Ancienne, white gold, manual wind, Piaget calibre 9P2, from 1999

**Piaget**
Polo, white gold, automatic, Piaget calibre 500P, from 1999

**Piaget**
Emperador retrograde second, white gold, automatic, Piaget calibre 560P, from 2006

**Piaget**
Altiplano ultrathin, white gold, manual wind, Piaget calibre 430P, from 2006

**Paul Picot**
Atelier 1100 Régulateur, steel, automatic, PP calibre 1100 (base calibre ETA 2892-A2), C.O.S.C. certified chronometer, power reserve display, from 1999

**Paul Picot**
Firshire 1937, white gold, manual wind, PP calibre 88 (base calibre ETA C735 from 1937), power reserve display, from 1999

This is something you should consider carefully before you ask the watchmaker to adjust a watch that is gaining maybe half a minute a week. Or if, after maybe three or five years of reliable service, a wristwatch needs a check-up and general service.

## The run to the banking and uneven teeth

The balance wheel receives an impulse from the fork of the escape lever, which brings it out of its resting position, and sets it in motion. At the same time the escape lever is caused to move towards the banking pins, after an escape tooth has given impulse to one of the pallets as it drops from the impulse face. Watchmakers call this movement the 'run to the banking'. In modern clocks, banking pins are generally no longer used. Instead, the anchor moves within a countersunk dip in the base plate.

The 'run to the banking' is also an important safety device in the escapement, because it

**Paul Picot**
Firshire Tonneau 3000 Retrograde, steel, automatic, PP calibre 1300 (base calibre ETA 2892-A2), from 1999

**Rado**
Anatom, tungsten-titanium carbide, automatic, ETA calibre 2671, from 1999

**Rado**
Original, steel, automatic, ETA calibre 2824-2, from 2006

**Rado**
Sintra XXL, ceramic, automatic, ETA calibre 2892-A2, from 2006

**Revue Thommen**
Specialties SK, steel, automatic, Revue Thommen calibre GT54, skeleton movement, from 2006

**Auguste Reymond**
Ragtime Power Reserve, steel,
automatic, AR calibre 9035 (base
calibre ETA 2892), power reserve
display, from 1999

**Auguste Reymond**
Boogie Gold Edition, red gold, manual
wind, ETA calibre 6425, from 2006

**Roamer**
Compétence Original Type 2, steel, manual
wind, FHF calibre 138.011, from 2006

## Rolex

Oyster Perpetual Milgauss, steel, automatic, Rolex calibre 1066M, C.O.S.C. certified chronometer, protected from magnetic fields by soft iron inner case, from 1958

## Rolex

Oyster Perpetual Chronometer, steel, automatic, Rolex calibre, also called the 'Bubble Back' because of its slightly domed base, from 1948

## Robergé

Andromède RS Régulateur, steel, automatic, Paul Picot calibre 1000 (base calibre Nouvelle Lémania), from 1999

## Rolex

Men's watch, yellow gold, manual wind, Rolex calibre, from 1930

## Rolex

Oyster Perpetual Chronometer, rose gold, automatic, Rolex calibre, also called the 'Bubble Back' because of its slightly domed base, with original Mickey Mouse face, from 1949

## Rolex

Prince Brancard Chronometer 'Extraprima Observatory Quality', steel, manual wind, Rolex calibre, from 1935

**Rolex**
Oyster Perpetual Air-King, steel, automatic, Rolex calibre 3130 (base calibre Rolex 3135), C.O.S.C. certified chronometer, from 2006

**Rolex**
Oyster Perpetual Day-Date, rose gold, automatic, Rolex calibre 3155 (base calibre Rolex 3135), C.O.S.C. certified chronometer, from 2006

guarantees that all the escape teeth can drop safely, even if they are not all of a uniform length. So if a tooth is a little too long, the escape lever is simply moved a little further, with the 'run to the banking' serving as additional manoeuvring room.

The oscillation amplitude of the balance wheel is, of course, dependent upon the impulse given to it; i.e. the balance wheel of a fully wound watch makes larger oscillations than those of a watch that has almost run down.

**Rolex**
Oyster Turn-O-Graph, steel, automatic, Rolex calibre 3135, C.O.S.C. certified chronometer, from 2006

**Rolex**
Prince Brancard Chronometer Jumping Hours, white gold, manual wind, jumping hour display, from 1945

**Rolex**
Prince, rose gold, manual wind, Rolex calibre 7040-2, C.O.S.C. certified chronometer, from 2006

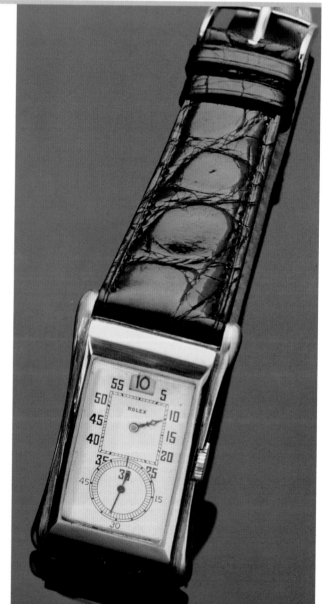

**Daniel Roth**

Rétrograde, yellow gold, manual wind, Lémania calibre 27NL reworked by Daniel Roth, from 1999

**Daniel Roth**

GMT, steel, automatic, Girard-Perregaux calibre GP 3100 reworked by Daniel Roth, second time zone digitally displayed, from 1999

**Jörg Schauer**

Day Date Zentral, steel, automatic, ETA calibre 2836, from 2006

**Jörg Schauer**

Digital 1, steel, automatic, PUW calibre 1560D, time displayed on three concentric dials, from 1999

**Jörg Schauer**

Kleine Schauer, steel, automatic, ETA calibre 2824, from 2006

### Otto Schlund

Classic with date display, steel, automatic,
ETA calibre 2824-2, from 2006

### Alain Silberstein

24 H, steel, automatic, base calibre ETA
2892-A2 reworked by Alain Silberstein,
24-hour time display, from 1999

### Stowa

Antea, steel, manual wind, ETA calibre
Peseux 7001, from 2006

### Seiko

Spring Drive, steel, automatic, Seiko calibre 5R65,
patented electromagnetic escapement system
'Tri-syncro regulator', from 2006

### Tissot

Men's watch, steel, manual wind,
calibre 20, from 1935

## When and why a clock goes accurately

One question that we haven't
answered yet: how do you make
a watch go faster or slower,
or, in an ideal world, just right?
Of course, this depends on
a wide variety of factors. The
basic requirements are a clean
and well-lubricated movement,
a mainspring that supplies as
constant a torque as possible, a
train with cleanly cut and perfectly
mounted wheels, an accurately
working escapement and of course
a well-adjusted balance made from

**Tissot**
Heritage Gold, red gold, automatic, ETA calibre 2895, C.O.S.C. certified chronometer, from 1999

**Ulysse Nardin**
San Marco Chronometer Venezia, yellow gold, automatic, base calibre ETA 2892, face made from cloisonné enamel, limited edition of 35 copies, from 1999

**Ulysse Nardin**
San Marco Chronometer Golden Hind, yellow gold, automatic, base calibre ETA 2892, face made from cloisonné enamel, limited edition of 25 copies, from 1999

**Ulysse Nardin**
Maxi Marine Chronometer, red gold, automatic, Ulysse Nardin calibre UN 26 (base calibre ETA 2892), C.O.S.C. certified chronometer, from 1999

**Ulysse Nardin**
Marine Chronometer, yellow gold, automatic, Ulysse Nardin calibre UN 26 (base calibre ETA 2892), C.O.S.C. certified chronometer, from 1999

non-magnetizable materials that are barely susceptible to changes in temperature.

Particularly high-quality watches that fulfil these requirements perfectly are regulated only with two tiny screws or small adjusting weights that are set into the balance rim, and are pulled out a little when the watch is going too fast, or twisted in when too slow. Examples of this are the Gyromax balance by Patek Philippe and the MicroStella screws on the Rolex balances.

## Curb pins and hands

However, most clocks rely on a different method of regulation, which uses curb pins and a regulator. So that the watchmaker can carry out

**Union**
Tradition Automatic, steel,
automatic, Union calibre 26-11,
from 1999

**Union**
Tradition Regulator, steel,
automatic, Union calibre 26-42,
from 1999

**Urban Jürgensen &
Sønner**
Referenz 5, yellow gold, automatic,
from 1999

**Union**
Classic Power Reserve, steel,
automatic, Union calibre
26-44, from 2006

**Urban Jürgensen &
Sønner**
Referenz 6, yellow gold, manual wind,
from 1999

71

**Vacheron Constantin**
Men's watch, red gold, manual wind,
Vacheron Constantin calibre,
from 1933

**Vacheron Constantin**
Automatic men's watch, red gold, manual wind, Vacheron
Constantin calibre 1072, from 1963

**Vacheron Constantin**
Les Historiques Rectangle, yellow gold, manual wind, Vacheron
Constantin calibre 1017, from 1999

**Vacheron Constantin**
Overseas, steel, automatic, Vacheron Constantin calibre
1310, from 1999

**Vacheron Constantin**
Montre à volets, yellow and white
gold, manual wind, blind in front of
the face operated by a second crown
at the nine o'clock position, Vacheron
Constantin calibre, from 1930

very slight adjustments to the regulation, many
watches feature what is known as a regulator
hand. This is located opposite the curb pins, and
it and the regulator are generally made from a
single piece of metal or held together by
friction.

The regulator hand, the regulator and the curb
pins work according to the same principle as
the two-armed lever. This means that the
watchmaker has to push the regulator hand in
the opposite direction to that which he requires
for the curb pins. This is generally simplified by
the + and − symbols or letters 'A' and 'R' milled
into the balance cock, whereby A (from the
French, avancer, meaning advance) makes the
watch run faster and R (from the French,
retarder, meaning delay) makes it run slower.

**Vacheron Constantin**

Toledo 1952, white gold, automatic, Vacheron Constantin calibre 1125, full calendar with moon phase display, from 2006

**Vacheron Constantin**

Overseas, steel, automatic, Vacheron Constantin calibre 1126, from 2006

**Vacheron Constantin**

Les Complications Saltarello, white gold, automatic, Vacheron Constantin calibre 1120MR, jumping hour hand display, retrograde minute display, from 1999

**Vulcain**

Men's watch, silver, manual wind, from 1925

**Raymond Weil**
Classic, steel, automatic, ETA calibre
2824-2, from 1999

**Zenith**
Port-Royal Chronometer, steel,
manual wind, Zenith calibre 135,
from 1965

**Raymond Weil**
Parsifal Réserve de Marche, steel,
automatic, RW calibre 3500 (base
calibre ETA 2892-A2), from 2006

**Raymond Weil**
Parsifal Automatic, steel, automatic,
ETA 2824-2, from 1999

**Zenith**
Chronomaster Elite HW, steel, manual wind, Zenith calibre 684 Elite, power reserve display, from 1999

**Xemex**
Offroad, steel, automatic, ETA calibre 2824-2, from 1999

**Xemex**
Avenue, steel, automatic, ETA calibre 2892-A2, from 1999

**Zenith**
Port-Royal Rectangle Elite, steel, automatic, Zenith calibre 684 Elite, from 2006

Occasionally the abbreviations 'F' and 'S' for 'fast' and 'slow' are also used.

There are various design features that make it easier to carry out very slight adjustments to the regulation of a watch; for instance, extremely long regulator hands (large displacement on the hand – small displacement on the regulator). Adjustment of the regulator might also be done by direct or indirect use of a micrometer screw (swan's neck fine regulaton device). Incidentally, a watch that gains five minutes a day is working very accurately. It just needs to be precisely regulated.

# 2. CHRONO-GRAPHS

A chronograph saves having to take constant glances at a watch when measuring short intervals of time. And when the timing of sporting events was still done by hand, it was also an extremely practical tool. Today the chronograph is first and foremost a sophisticated men's toy, useful, for instance, for checking the grilling time for steaks. However, watchmakers and watch designers still devote enormous amounts of effort to it.

**Angelus**
Chronograph, yellow gold, manual
wind with column wheel operation,
from 1945

**Audemars Piguet**
Chronograph, yellow gold, manual
wind with column wheel operation,
from 1949

**Audemars Piguet**
Royal Oak Offshore Chronograph,
steel, automatic, AP calibre
2226/2840, from 2006

**Baume & Mercier**
CapeLand, steel, automatic,
ETA calibre 7750, from 1999

**Baume & Mercier**
Classima Chronograph, steel,
automatic, BM calibre 13283 (base
calibre Lémania 283), from 1999

**Baume & Mercier**
Malibu Chronograph, steel,
automatic, BM calibre 13750 (base
calibre ETA 750), from 1999

**Baume & Mercier**
Milleis Chronograph, rose gold,
manual wind, calibre Lémania 1870,
from 1999

With the invention of the clock, man fulfilled his desire to divide the time of the day into periods that were as even as possible. This ambition satisfied, in the nineteenth century he began to aspire towards being able to measure and even record short intervals of time, irrespective of the time of day.

You can, of course, measure a journey from A to B by constantly looking at your watch. But this is extremely inconvenient and not without its dangers if sitting behind the steering wheel.

Fortunately for us, inventive watchmakers have provided us with as practical an instrument as

the chronograph for just such a contingency, a tool that enables us to measure a short period of time by simply pressing a button, without needing to pay too much attention.

## Time writer without a writing instrument

The term chronograph comes from the Greek and is formed from the stems Chronos (time) and Graphô (I write). Now, you could justifiably argue that the term Chrono-'Graph' is no longer appropriate for today's watches with integral stopwatches, because these watches are used for neither writing nor recording. But remember that we also still talk about

'steamers', even though large ships have been powered by diesel engines or gas turbines for decades, and that it's a long time since a car's 'mudguards' have carried out the function implied by their name. The first chronograph really was a time writer. In 1820, the French watchmaker, Rieussec, invented a watch that wrote on the watch face with an ink pen secured to the hand, when a mechanism was activated.

In 1831, Austrian-born watchmaker Joseph Thaddäus Winnerl, a former employee of the watchmaking genius, Abraham Louis Breguet, who had died in 1823, invented a watch, the second hand of which could be stopped and restarted whenever required, independently of the clockwork movement. A crucial drawback of Winnerl's design was the extremely slow return of the second hand to the zero position at the end of a measurement.

In 1862, this problem was overcome by Adolphe Nicole from the Joux Valley (French Switzerland), who developed and patented the first chronographs with hands that could be instantly reset. To achieve this, Nicole fixed a heart-shaped cam on to the arbour of the second hand.

When the chronograph hand was reset to zero, a spring-loaded lever operated laterally against this cam, which has remained virtually unchanged to the present day, and because of its characteristic shape is known by watchmakers simply as the 'heart piece'. When struck by the impact of this 'violent' lever, the heart piece is forced to reverberate back and forth until the flats of the heart cams rest against the heart piece lever.

**Bertolucci**
Vir Chronograph, steel, automatic, ETA calibre 7750, from 1999

**Baume & Mercier**
CapeLand S Chronograph, steel, automatic, BM calibre 13750 (base calibre ETA 7750), from 2006

**Blancpain**
Chronograph 2100, yellow gold, automatic, from 1999

Masculine characteristics: an arrangement of high-quality chronographs from Officine Panerai, Zenith and Blancpain

**Blancpain**
Léman Chrono Fly-Back Large Date, steel, automatic, Blancpain calibre 69F8, from 2006

## Fourth wheel – second purpose

The chronograph mechanism is generally driven by the fourth wheel.

There are various options for transferring the power from the fourth wheel, which rotates within the actual movement, i.e. between the plates, to the chronograph movement. In the traditional design the chronograph movement is situated on the rear wheel train bridge, so is outside the actual clock movement.

A common method for transmitting the drive is by mounting two long pivots on to the arbour of the fourth wheel (turning within the movement). There is already one pivot on the dial side of the movement, which carries the little second hand. On the second long pivot, which projects from the wheel train bridge, a removable clamp is used to attach another wheel, the driving wheel. Unlike the wheels of the actual movement, this wheel has triangular teeth. Drive is transmitted via wheels that interlock with each other, as opposed to wheels engaging with pinions, the usual action in a wheel train.

The external driving wheel, the one that is mounted on to the arbour of the fourth wheel, engages with another wheel (the coupling clutch wheel) with the same teeth, which sits on a moving lever called the coupling clutch lever.

The coupling clutch lever can rotate slightly round a pivot above the wheel train bridge. A second pivot with a large head and a lug beneath it, which is bolted into the mechanism plate via an oval hole in the coupling lever, determines the range of movement. A small spring (the coupling clutch spring) pushes the coupling lever towards the centre. This results in the wheel on top of it – the coupling wheel – meshing with the chronograph centre wheel, the teeth of which are only half the size, but identically shaped. So when the start button on the watchcase is pressed, the blocking lever moves out of the way. At the same time, the

**Rainer Brand**
Carcassonne, steel, automatic,
Lémania calibre 1352, from 1999

**Rainer Brand**
Kerala, steel, automatic, ETA calibre
7750, from 2006

**Breguet**
Split-Second Chronograph, yellow
gold, manual wind, Breguet calibre
533 NT, from 1999

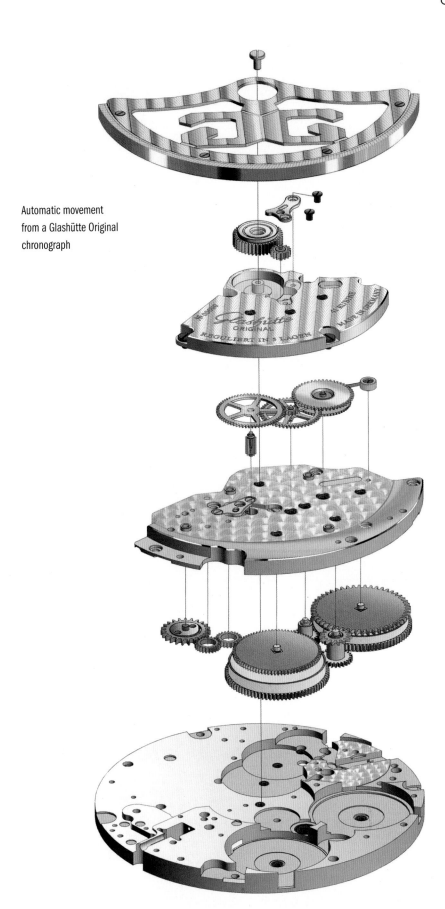

Automatic movement
from a Glashütte Original
chronograph

**Breguet**
Marine Chronograph, platinum,
manual wind, Breguet calibre 576,
from 1999

**Breguet**
Heritage Chronograph, steel,
automatic, Breguet calibre 550,
from 2006

83

**Breitling**
Chronograph Pupitre Reference
7101.3, steel, manual wind, Valjoux
calibre 7750, from 1975

**Breitling**
Chronograph Football
Reference 2734.3, steel,
manual wind, Valjoux calibre
7731, from 1975

**Breitling**
Split-Seconds Chronograph
Reference 762, steel, manual wind,
with 45-minute counter, from 1950

**Breitling**
Chronograph Sprint Reference 2018,
steel, manual wind, Valjoux calibre
7733, from 1975

**Breitling**
Chrono-Matic Reference 2112-15,
steel, automatic, calibre 15,
from 1969

**Breitling**
Crosswind, steel, automatic,
Breitling calibre 13 (base
calibre ETA 7750), from 1999

**Breitling**
Montbrillant Olympus, steel,
automatic, Breitling calibre 19 (base
calibre ETA 2892-A2), from 2006

**Bulova**
Doctor's Watch, steel/gold-plated,
manual wind, FHF calibre 138.001,
from 1999

**Breitling**
Chronomat Evolution, steel,
automatic, Breitling calibre 13 (base
calibre ETA 7750), C.O.S.C. certified
chronometer, from 2006

**Bunz**
Chronograph, platinum, automatic,
ETA calibre 7750, from 2006

**Bvlgari**

Assioma Chrono, yellow gold, automatic, ETA calibre 2094, from 2006

**Cartier**

Pasha de Cartier, steel, automatic, Cartier calibre 205 (base calibre Frédéric Piguet 1185), from 1999

**Bvlgari**

Bvlgari Rattrapante, yellow gold, automatic, Bvlgari calibre MVA 900 (base calibre GP 8290), from 1999

coupling lever moves towards the centre, causing the coupling wheel to engage the chronograph centre wheel. The chronograph begins its task of measuring a short interval of time. This design enables the chronograph mechanism to be turned on and off as required.

If the interval being measured lasts for longer than one minute, the minutes counting wheel, which operates the 30-minute counter in front of the clock's dial, has to be advanced by one step. To do this, an arm, which is also mounted on to the arbour of the chronograph centre wheel, meshes with the teeth of the intermediate wheel, which in turn interlocks with the minutes counting wheel. The intermediate wheel is advanced by one tooth. Because they have the same teething, the minutes counting wheel also advances by one tooth. At the same time, on the other side of the works, on the front of the dial, the hand of the 30-minute counter advances by exactly one graduation mark.

This is facilitated by a small locking spring (minute count-wheel spring), which meshes with

## Cartier

Roadster Chronograph, steel/yellow gold, automatic, Cartier calibre 8510 (base calibre ETA 2894), from 2006

## Certina

DS 2 Chronolympic, steel, manual wind, calibre Valjoux 726, from 1975

## Certina

DS-3 Chronograph, steel, automatic, Certina calibre 674 (base calibre ETA 7750), from 2006

## Philippe Charriol

Supersports Chronograph, steel, automatic, ETA calibre 7750, from 1999

## Chopard

Imperiale Chronograph, steel, automatic, Lémania calibre 283, from 1999

87

**Chronoswiss**

Chronograph-Chronometer, steel, automatic, Chronoswiss calibre C.754 (base calibre ETA 7750), from 1999

**Chronoswiss**

Classic Chronograph, steel, automatic, Chronoswiss calibre C.741 (base calibre ETA 7750), from 2006

Optical delectation: Chronoswiss Chronoscope with visible column wheel, reference number CH 1523 rc, from 2006

**Chronoswiss**

Pathos, platinum, automatic, Chronoswiss calibre C.732S (base calibre ETA 7750), movement completely skeletized, from 2006

the teeth of the minutes counting wheel, only allowing it to advance by one tooth. Finally the wheel is held exactly in position by the minute count-wheel spring until the chronograph centre wheel again 'sweeps' all the wheels along.

At the end of the timing process, another button is pushed, the coupling lever jumps back, releases its mesh and the blocking lever moves against the chronograph wheel to stop it.

**Du Bois & Fils**
Chronographe Classique, yellow gold,
manual wind, Nouvelle Lémania
calibre 1873, from 2006

**Cyma**
Chronograph, silver, manual wind,
from 1920

**Corum**
Classical Fly-Back Big Date, steel, automatic,
calibre CO 996 (base calibre ETA 2892-A2),
C.O.S.C. certified chronometer, from 2006

**De Bethune**
Monokrone Chronograph, white gold, manual wind, calibre
DB 5008 (base calibre LIP 5000), chronograph push
button in the crown, from 2006

**Dior**
Chiffre Rouge Chronograph A02, steel,
automatic, ETA calibre 2894-2, from 2006

**Dubey & Schaldenbrand**
Trial, rose gold, automatic, ETA
calibre 7750 with Tricompax display,
from 1999

**Dubey & Schaldenbrand**
Fly-Back, rose gold, automatic,
ETA calibre 7750 with split-second
chronograph design, from 1999

**Dubey & Schaldenbrand**
Aerochrono, rose gold, automatic,
ETA calibre 2094, from 2006

**Roger Dubuis**
S.A.W. Easy Diver, steel, manual wind,
RD calibre 56, from 2006

**Ebel**
Le Modulor, steel, automatic, Ebel calibre 137,
C.O.S.C. certified chronometer, from 1999

**Ebel**
1911 Chronograph, rose gold,
automatic, Ebel calibre 137, C.O.S.C.
certified chronometer, from 2006

**Eberhard**
Replica 2 Counter, silver/gold-plated, manual wind, Lémania calibre 1872, from 1999

**Eberhard**
Split-Second Chronograph
Extra-fort, yellow gold, manual wind with dual column wheel operation, from 1945

**Eberhard**
Chronomaster, steel, one-way bezel, automatic, Lémania calibre 5100, from 1999

**Eberhard**
Tazio Nuvolari, steel, automatic, ETA calibre 7750, from 1999

**Eberhard**
Chrono 4, steel, automatic, calibre
EB 200 (base calibre ETA 2894-2),
from 2006

## The oscillating pinion

Because this chronograph mechanism is technically complicated and therefore expensive to produce, Edouard Heuer (founder of the Heuer watch brand, which is manufactured under the TAG Heuer name nowadays) invented what is called the oscillating pinion, for which he received a patent in May 1887. This oscillating pinion consists of an arbour with two separate toothed wheel rims. The teeth on the dial side engage with the movement's fourth wheel (bearing the seconds hand), and those on the opposite side with the chronograph centre wheel. To engage (start) or disengage (stop) the

**Eberhard**
Quadrangolo Chrono Screen, steel, manual wind,
Lémania 1872, from 1999

**Eterna**
Porsche Design Chronograph, steel,
automatic, ETA calibre 7750,
from 1999

**Eterna**
25-year Porsche Design Chronograph,
steel, automatic, ETA calibre 7750,
from 1999

**Eterna**
Pulsometer Chronograph, yellow gold,
automatic, ETA calibre 2894-2,
from 1999

**Eterna**
1948 Moon Phase Chronograph,
steel, automatic, ETA calibre 7751,
certified chronometer, from 2006

**Jacques Etoile**
Monaco 72C, steel, manual wind,
Valjoux calibre 72C, from 2006

**Jacques Etoile**
Silverstone Valjoux 23, sterling silver,
manual wind, Valjoux calibre 23,
from 2006

**Formex**
Chrono-Tacho, steel/titanium,
automatic, ETA calibre 7754,
glass-covered slide rule bezel,
from 2006

**Girard-Perregaux**
Richeville Tonneau Chronograph, red
gold, manual wind, Girard-Perregaux
calibre 8381, from 1999

**Girard-Perregaux**
Doctor's Chronograph, yellow gold,
manual wind, calibre 281, from 1940

**Gérald Genta**
Gefica Chronograph, bronze, automatic,
ETA calibre 7750, from 1999

teeth, the oscillating pinion is lightly tilted. Today, this ingenious design is as popular as ever – after all, it is used by today's most widely sold chronograph movement, the ETA 7750 (Valjoux).

## Controlled heartbeat

We now reach the last stage in the timing process: resetting to zero. The second case pusher is activated and pushes against the reset-to-zero lever. The chronograph centre wheel is released by the brake, which holds it when it is not engaged with the coupling wheel.

The heart piece lever is released and is catapulted by the heart piece spring against the heart pieces on the centre wheel and the minutes counting wheel. The wheels jerk into the reset position and are held at zero by the hammers of the heart piece lever. These switching operations take place in a fraction of a second, but certainly not at the same time. If,

**Girard-Perregaux**
Vintage III, red gold, automatic, Girard-Perregaux calibre 3170, from 1999

**Girard-Perregaux**
GP 7000 Américaine Chronograph, steel/yellow gold, automatic, Girard-Perregaux calibre 8000, from 1999

**Girard-Perregaux**
Ferrari 250 GT TdF, steel, automatic, Girard-Perregaux calibre 2280, 24-hour display, from 1999

**Girard-Perregaux**
Ferrari Chronograph Carbon, steel, automatic, Girard-Perregaux calibre 2280, from 1999

**Girard-Perregaux**
Ferrari Chronograph, steel,
automatic, Girard-Perregaux calibre
2280, from 1999

**Girard-Perregaux**
Laureato EVO 3, steel, automatic, GP calibre 33CD-AOWA,
24-hour display (dual time zone), from 2006

**Girard-Perregaux**
Richeville Chronograph Carbon, red gold, automatic,
GP calibre 3370 (base calibre GP 3300), from 2006

### Glashütte Original

Senator Chronograph, steel, automatic, Glashütte Original
calibre 39-30, from 1999

Far right: Watches from small manufacturers can also be
technically and visually impressive. Best example: chronographs
from Graham and Temption.

**Girard-Perregaux**
Ferrari Chronograph F50, steel,
automatic, Girard-Perregaux calibre
3170, perpetual calendar, 24-hour
display, from 1999

for example, the heart piece lever were to strike
the heart piece before the brake had disengaged
from the centre wheel, the brake, still lying
in its engaged position, might damage the
extremely fine teeth on the wheel.

The adjustment of the wheels and levers and
their mesh with each other is made by turning
eccentrical screws to adjust the distance of the
parts from each other. This calibration is done
under strong magnification, preferably using
a microscope.

**Glashütte Original**

Senator Chronograph Date, steel, automatic, Glashütte Original calibre 39-32, from 1999

**Glashütte Original**

Sport Chronograph Senator, steel, automatic, Glashütte Original calibre 10-60, from 1999

**Glashütte Original**

PanoMaticChrono, steel, manual wind, Glashütte Original calibre 61, chronograph with Fly-Back function, from 1999

**Glashütte Original**

PanoRetroGraph, rose gold, manual wind, Glashütte Original calibre 60, chronograph with Fly-Back reset function, from 2006

**Glashütte Original**

Sport Evolution Chronograph, steel, automatic, Glashütte Original calibre 39-31, from 2006

## Graham

Chronofighter Classic, steel, automatic, Graham calibre 1722 (base calibre ETA 7750), release lever on crown for chronograph operation, certified chronometer, from 2006

## Graham

Swordfish, steel, automatic, Graham calibre 1726 (base calibre ETA 7750), also with crown and pusher on left side of casing, from 2006

## Gucci

G Chrono, steel, quartz, ETA calibre 251.471H1, from 2006

## Hanhart

Sirius Chronograph, steel, automatic, ETA calibre 7750, from 2006

99

**Michel Herbelin**
Newport J-Class Chronograph Fly-Back, steel, automatic, LIP calibre 8151 (base calibre ETA 7750), from 2006

**Heuer**
Calculator, steel, rotating bezel with slide rule scale, automatic, calibre 12 with microrotor, from 1975

**Heuer**
Montreal, steel, automatic, calibre 12 with microrotor, from 1975

**Heuer**
Autavia, steel, automatic, calibre 12 with microrotor, from 1975

## Triangular pillars as switches

Of course, there have been considerable advances in the development of chronograph technology. For instance, over the last ten years, the cost factor has led to the introduction of various chronograph modules that are mounted on to the dial side of the movement.

Unfortunately, and much to the regret of devotees of the classic chronograph, this has resulted in one elaborate detail or another falling victim to the simplified mechanism. These details include the column wheel which, however, in keeping with the recent return to the sophisticated design of earlier chronographs, is reappearing in newly designed modules.

There have always been chronographs without a column wheel, which, from an economical point of view, are preferable to the more sophisticated column wheel designs. However, the chronographs were always mounted on the reverse side of the movement. The column

**Heuer**
Monaco, steel, automatic, calibre 12 with microrotor, from 1975

**Hublot**
Chronograph Automatic, platinum,
automatic, Frédéric Piguet calibre
1188, from 1999

TAG Heuer calibre 360

**Hublot**
Big Bang, steel, automatic, calibre
HUB 44 (developed and produced by
La Joux Perret), from 2006

## Ikepod

Isopod Chronograph, steel, automatic, ETA calibre 2894-2, C.O.S.C. certified chronometer, from 1999

## Ikepod

Hemipode Chronograph, steel, automatic, ETA calibre 7750, 24-hour display, C.O.S.C. certified chronometer, from 1999

## IWC

Portuguese Chrono Rattrapante, red gold, automatic, IWC calibre C.76240 (base calibre ETA 7750 with IWC split-second design), from 1999

## IWC

Portuguese Chrono Automatic, steel, automatic, IWC calibre C.79240 (base calibre ETA 7750), from 1999

wheel – or pillar wheel – design still rates as the crème de la crème of chronograph mechanisms. The term column wheel derives from the French word *colonne* (column or pillar). The column wheel coordinates all the other switching functions in the watch's chronograph mechanism. In this design the pillars stand to attention like files on a revolving shelf, on top of a wheel with saw-teething on the wheel train bridge of the chronograph.

The column wheel coordinates the starting, stopping, and reset-to-zero functions of the chronograph. When the start pusher, located on the case near the two o'clock position, is pressed, the operating lever gives the column wheel the order 'to advance by one tooth'. To carry out the order a small hook on the operating lever meshes with the saw-teeth of the column wheel and rotates it round by one tooth, whereupon a powerful blocking spring fixes the new position.

At the same time a beak on the coupling lever, with which the connection to the wheel train is made, alternately engages or disengages between the triangular columns.

**IWC**
Engineer Chronograph, steel, IWC calibre 79350 (base calibre ETA 7750), from 2006

**Daniel JeanRichard**
Chronograph Sport Tachymeter, steel, automatic, calibre DJR 25 (base calibre ETA 2824-2), from 1999

**Jaeger-LeCoultre**
Master Chrono, steel, quartz with mechanical chronograph function, from 1999

**Jaeger-LeCoultre**
Master Compressor Chronograph, steel, automatic, JLC calibre 751, from 2006

**Daniel JeanRichard**
Chronograph Classic, steel, automatic, calibre DJR 25 (base calibre ETA 2824-2), from 1999

**Daniel JeanRichard**
TV Screen Chronograph, steel,
automatic, calibre DJR 25 (base
calibre ETA 2824-2), from 1999

**Junghans**
Tourneur Chronograph,
steel, automatic,
ETA calibre 7750,
from 1999

**Junghans**
Chronograph, steel,
manual wind, calibre 88,
from 1950

**Daniel JeanRichard**
TV Screen Chronoscope, steel,
automatic, JR calibre 25 (base
calibre ETA 2824-2), bidirectional
rotating inner bezel, from 2006

**Junghans**
Arthur Junghans Ambassador,
gold-plated steel, automatic,
ETA calibre 7750, from 2006

If the coupling lever receives the order to 'engage', it slips its beak into the gap between two of the (generally) seven columns on the column wheel. This creates the link between the wheels within the motion work and the chronograph mechanism.

If the start pusher is pressed again the first part of the operation is repeated; however, this time the beak on the coupling lever is raised up by one of the triangular pillars and disengages the link between the column wheel and the chronograph centre wheel. Due to the action of the blocking lever and the minute count-wheel spring, the chronograph hands

**Kurth**
Chronograph Venus, rose gold,
manual wind, Venus calibre
187, from 1999

**Maurice Lacroix**
Column wheel chronograph, yellow
gold, manual wind, calibre ML 83
(base calibre Valjoux 23), from 1999

**Kelek**
Chronograph, steel, automatic, Kelek calibre 2060
(base calibre ETA 2892-A2) from 1999

**Kurth**
Paris Chronograph, yellow
gold, automatic, ETA calibre
7750, from 2006

**Krieger**
Aficionado Chronoscope, steel,
automatic, ETA calibre 7750,
from 1999

**Maurice Lacroix**
Chronograph Réserve de Marche,
steel/yellow gold, automatic, calibre
ML 30 (base calibre ETA 7750),
from 1999

**Maurice Lacroix**
Croneo, steel, automatic, ETA calibre 7750, from 1999

**Maurice Lacroix**
Pontos Chronograph, steel, automatic, ML calibre 111 (base calibre ETA 7750), from 2006

**Maurice Lacroix**
Masterpiece Venus, white gold, manual wind, ML calibre 36 (base calibre Venus 175), from 2006

**A. Lange & Söhne**
Datograph, platinum, manual wind, Lange calibre L951.1, from 2006

**A. Lange & Söhne**
Double Split, platinum, manual wind, Lange calibre L001.1, two column wheels for operating rattrapante Fly-Back function, from 2006

**A. Lange & Söhne**
1815 Chronograph, white gold, manual wind, Lange calibre L951.0, from 2006

**Lémania**
Chronograph, steel, manual wind with column wheel operation, from 1940

**Limes**
Integral Chrono, steel, automatic, ETA calibre 7750, from 2006

**Locman**
Panorama, rose gold, automatic, ETA calibre 2894-2, from 2006

**Longines**
Chronograph, steel, manual wind, calibre 13ZN, from 1944

**Longines**
Chronograph, nickel, manual wind with column wheel operation, from 1925

remain where they are until the pusher at the four o'clock position is pressed, and then all of the chronograph hands return to zero.

## The split-second hand

There is no other kind of watch that bears as many different names for the pièce de résistance of chronograph design: it's called a rattrapante, a split-second chronograph, or simply a double-handed chronograph. The 'double' refers to the chronograph centre seconds hand. During normal chronograph operation, both seconds hands run so exactly on top of each other that at first glance they appear to be just one hand.

The technical ingenuity of this design rests in the way that one of the hands can be stopped independently of the other and then catch its twin up with one jump. The translation for 'catch up' in French is *rattraper*. So this stopwatch function is generally termed 'rattrapante'. Sometimes the term double chronograph is used, though this is not quite as

**Longines**
Lindbergh Spirit Chronograph, steel/yellow gold, bidirectional rotating bezel for measuring degree of longitude, automatic, Longines calibre L674.8 (base calibre ETA 7750), from 1999

**Longines**

Francillon Split-Second Chronograph,
yellow gold, automatic, Longines calibre
L668.2 (base calibre ETA 7750),
from 1999

**Longines**

Avigation Chronograph, steel,
automatic, Longines calibre L651
(base calibre ETA 2894-2), from 1999

**Longines**

Francillon Chronograph, steel,
automatic, Longines calibre L667
(base calibre ETA 7750), from 1999

**Longines**

Master Collection Chronograph,
steel, automatic, Longines
calibre L651 (base calibre
ETA 2894-2), special edition
Olympia, from 2006

accurate a description; a more common name is a split-second chronograph, and it is also occasionally described as a tow-hand.

The name refers to the fact that the 'tow-hand' is normally dragged along – towed – round the dial by its twin brother. The particular feature of these watches is the third push-piece that is generally located on the left-hand side of the case or in the winding crown. Its sole purpose is to stop or release the second chronograph hand.

In contrast to their operation, the use of these watches can be quickly explained: take, for instance, two athletes competing over a set distance. To record the different times for the runners you would normally need two stopwatches – or alternatively one chronograph with a tow-hand. This has the further benefit that the race results cannot be fudged by pushing one start button after the other. When the starting signal is given, the chronograph

**Longines**
Master Collection Chronograph, steel, automatic, Longines calibre L651 (base calibre ETA 2894-2), from 2006

**Minerva**
Heritage, steel, manual wind, calibre Venus 175, from 1999

**Minerva**
Chronograph Antimagnetic, yellow gold, manual wind with column wheel operation, from 1940

**Longines**
Tonneau Chronograph, steel, automatic, Longines calibre L667 (base calibre ETA 7750), from 1999

**Mido**
All Dial Chrono Chronometer, steel, automatic, Mido calibre 1320 (base calibre ETA 7750), from 2006

**Minerva**
Chronograph Athena II, sterling silver,
automatic, ETA calibre 7750,
from 1999

**Movado**
Chronograph, steel, manual wind,
calibre Movado C 95M, full calendar
with moon phase display, from 1950

**Montblanc**
Masterpiece
Chronograph, yellow
gold, automatic,
ETA 7750, from 1999

**Movado**
Datron HS360, steel, automatic,
calibre 3019PHC (base calibre
Zenith 400 El Primero), from 1975

**Minerva**
Palladio Nostalgia, steel,
automatic, ETA calibre 7750,
from 1999

### Mühle Glashütte
Teutonia II Chronograph, steel, automatic, ETA calibre 7750, from 2006

### Franck Muller
Conquistador Chronograph, red gold, automatic, Franck Muller calibre 1185 (base calibre Frédéric Piguet 11.85), from 1999

### Franck Muller
Cintrée Curvex Casablanca Chronograph, steel, automatic, FM calibre 7002 CO (base calibre ETA 7750), from 2006

### Franck Muller
Cintrée Curvex Chronograph Havana, yellow gold, automatic, Franck Muller calibre 1185 (base calibre Frédéric Piguet 11.85), from 1999

### Franck Muller
Master City, red gold, automatic, Franck Muller calibre 7000 (base calibre ETA 7750), from 1999

### Franck Muller
Cintrée Curvex Chronograph Birétrograde, white gold, automatic, FM calibre 7000 B, from 2006

**Omega**
Speedmaster Broad Arrow, steel, automatic, Omega calibre 3303, C.O.S.C. certified chronometer, from 2006

### Nivrel
Chronograph Large Minute Hand, steel, automatic, ETA calibre 2892-2 with Dubois-Dépraz chronograph module 2073, from 1999

**Omega**
Chronograph, steel, manual wind, calibre 33.3 CHRO T6, with column wheel operation, from 1938

**Omega**
Chronograph, yellow gold, manual wind, calibre 28.1 CHRO T1, one-pusher chronograph with column wheel operation, from 1939

**Omega**
Seamaster Professional Chrono Diver, titanium/tantalum/red gold, unidirectional rotating bezel with dive scale, automatic, Omega calibre 1164 (base calibre ETA 7750), C.O.S.C. certified chronometer, from 1999

**Omega**
De Ville Co-Axial Chronograph Rattrapante, steel, automatic, Omega calibre 3612 (base calibre 3303), C.O.S.C. certified chronometer, from 2006

**Omega**
Speedmaster Professional Mark II, steel, manual wind, calibre 861, from 1968

Omega De Ville Co-Axial Chronograph Rattrapante, from 2006

**Omega**
Speedmaster Professional, steel,
manual wind, Omega calibre 1863
(base calibre Lémania 1873),
from 1999

**Omega**
Speedmaster Day-Date, steel,
automatic, Omega calibre 1151 (base
calibre ETA 7751), from 1999

button at the two o'clock position on the watchcase is pushed, and both athletes and hands set off. When the first runner crosses the finishing line, the rattrapante push-piece in the crown or left-hand side of the case is pressed and the tow-hand (A) stops. When the second runner crosses the finishing line the chronograph is stopped in the usual manner, the sweep hand (B) also stops and the times of both runners can be read off.

Repeated pressing of the rattrapante push-piece enables successive intervals to be timed. For example, if one wished to measure a longer run

113

## Omega
Dynamic Chrono, steel, automatic, Omega calibre 1138 (base calibre ETA 2890-02), from 1999

## Oris
Williams F1 Chronograph, black/PVD-coated stainless steel, automatic, Oris calibre 673 (base calibre ETA 7750), from 2006

## Patek Philippe
Eternal Calendar Chronograph, platinum, manual wind, Patek Philippe calibre CH 27-70, from 1999

## Panerai
Luminor 1950 Rattrapante, steel, automatic, Panerai calibre OP XVIII, C.O.S.C. certified chronometer, from 2006

## Oris
Big Crown Chronograph, Oris calibre 674 (base calibre ETA 2824-2), from 1999

with short breaks, the tow-hand would be stopped several times and read off, and when the push-piece was pressed again, the tow-hand would catch up with the principal chronograph hand.

**Patek Philippe**
Waterproof Chronograph, rose gold, manual wind, calibre 13-30 with column wheel operation, from 1953

**Paul Picot**
Atelier Split-Second Chronograph, platinum, manual wind, Paul Picot calibre PP310 (base calibre Venus 179), from 1999

**Paul Picot**
Firshire Tonneau Chronograph, stainless steel, manual wind, ETA calibre 2892-2, from 1999

**Péquignet**
Mooréa Chronograph Tonneau, stainless steel/yellow gold, automatic, ETA calibre 2894, from 1999

**Péquignet**
Mooréa Chronograph, stainless steel/yellow gold, automatic, ETA calibre 2824-2 with Dubois-Dépraz chronograph module, C.O.S.C. certified chronometer, from 1999

**Paul Picot**
Le Chronograph Mythique, stainless
steel/yellow gold, automatic,
modified ETA calibre 7750,
from 1999

**Porsche Design**
P 6612 PAC, aluminum/black PVD-
coating, automatic, ETA calibre
2894-2, from 2006

**Porsche Design**
P 6613 PGR, rose gold, automatic,
ETA calibre 7750 AR2, from 2006

## Hollow arbours for the hands and the heart piece is back again

In the rattrapante mechanism the first
chronograph centre wheel arbour rotates inside
the hollow minute wheel arbour, and the arbour
of the second chronograph centre wheel (split-
seconds wheel) rotates in the arbour of the
principal seconds wheel, which is likewise a
hollow tube.

During normal chronograph operation, a heart-
shaped cam that sits on the chronograph wheel
carries along the split-seconds wheel. A tiny
sprung lever (split-seconds lever) presses against
this cam. On the end of the lever is a tiny coil
that sits between the flats of the heart.
Meanwhile, the two seconds hands are sitting
exactly on top of one another and when the start
push-piece is pressed, they set off together.

**Paul Picot**
Technograph, stainless steel,
automatic, ETA calibre 7750,
from 2006

**Auguste Reymond**
Cotton Club Black Chrono, stainless steel, automatic, ETA calibre 7750, from 1999

**Auguste Reymond**
Jazz Age, yellow gold, automatic, ETA calibre 7751, moon phase display, from 2006

**Porsche Design**
Indicator, Titan, automatic, Porsche Design calibre (base calibre ETA 7750), elapsed minutes and seconds are displayed digitally, from 2006

**Robergé**
Andromède II Chronograph, stainless steel, quartz with mechanical chronograph module, base calibre Frédéric Piguet 1270, from 1999

**Rolex**
Oyster Cosmograph Daytona, stainless steel, manual wind, calibre 727, from 1979

**Robergé**
Andromède RS Chronograph, stainless steel, quartz with mechanical chronograph module, base calibre Frédéric Piguet 1270, from 1999

**Robergé**
M31 Chronograph, yellow gold, quartz with mechanical chronograph module, base calibre Frédéric Piguet 1270, from 1999

If the push-piece for the split-second hand is pressed, pincers reminiscent of those of a beetle grab the toothless rattrapante wheel and grip it firmly. The chronograph centre wheel continues to run, whilst the coil is gently pressed against the heart-shaped cam by the spring-powered lever.

If the rattrapante push-piece is pressed again, the sprung lever presses on the 'lowest' point of the cam, between the two flats of the heart, and the rattrapante wheel is instantly returned to its original position and brought into renewed synchrony with the principal chronograph hand.

**Rolex**
Oyster Chronograph Antimagnetic Jean-Claude Killy, stainless steel, manual wind, calibre 72C, full calendar, from 1954

**Rolex**

Oyster Chronograph 'Pre-Daytona', stainless steel, manual wind, calibre 722.1, from 1966

**Rolex**

Oyster Chronographs, all stainless steel and with manual wind mechanisms, left and right calibre R23, centre chronograph with full calendar, calibre Valjoux 72 C, from 1945 to 1950

**Rolex**

Oyster Perpetual Cosmograph Daytona, stainless steel/yellow gold, automatic, Rolex calibre 4130, from 2006

**Daniel Roth**

Manual wind Chronograph, white gold, base calibre Lémania NL 2310, reworked by Daniel Roth, from 1999

### Daniel Roth

Automatic Chronograph, stainless steel, base calibre Zenith 400 El Primero, reworked by Daniel Roth, from 1999

### Jörg Schauer

Quarada, stainless steel, automatic, ETA calibre 7750, from 2006

### Jörg Schauer

Chronograph Kulisse Edition I, stainless steel, automatic, ETA calibre 7750, reworked by Jörg Schauer, from 1999

### Scalfaro

Cap Ferrat Chrono Large Date Fly-Back, stainless steel, automatic, ADK calibre 151 (base calibre ETA 7750), bidirectional rotating inner bezel, from 2006

### Jörg Schauer

Chronograph Kulisse Edition 4, stainless steel, automatic, ETA calibre 7750 with design for 24-hour display, reworked by Jörg Schauer, from 1999

### Jörg Schauer

Chronograph Kulisse Edition 5, stainless steel, automatic, ETA calibre 7750 with split-second design, reworked by Jörg Schauer, from 1999

## Scalfaro

Porto Cervo Chronograph TriCompax, stainless steel, automatic, ADK calibre 150 (base calibre ETA 7750), from 2006

## Otto Schlund

Classic Chronograph, stainless steel, automatic, ETA calibre 7750, from 2006

## Alexander Shorokhoff

Leo Tolstoi, stainless steel, manual wind, Poljot calibre 3133, from 2006

## Schwarz Etienne

Fly-Back, stainless steel, automatic, LIP calibre 8151 (base calibre ETA 7750), from 2006

## Alain Silberstein

Krono A, stainless steel, automatic, Frédéric Piguet calibre 1185, reworked by Alain Silberstein, from 1999

**Alain Silberstein**
Krono B, stainless steel, automatic,
Lémania calibre 5100, reworked by
Alain Silberstein, from 1999

**Alain Silberstein**
Bolido Krono Carbonfibre, stainless steel, automatic, Frédéric
Piguet calibre 1185, reworked by Alain Silberstein, from 2006

**Sinn**
Gold Chronograph, yellow gold, automatic, ETA calibre 7750,
C.O.S.C. certified chronometer, from 1999

**Alain Silberstein**
Krono Bauhaus 2 Woodland,
stainless steel/Cloisonné-lacquered,
automatic, ETA calibre 7751,
from 1999

**Sinn**
303 Kristall Yukon Quest
Chronograph, stainless steel,
dehumidifying capsule
screwed into case, cold-
resistant special oil,
automatic, ETA calibre 7750,
from 1999

**Sinn**
Navigation chronograph, stainless steel/gold-plated,
manual wind, Lémania calibre 1873, from 1999

122

**Sinn**
The classic/sporty Chronograph, stainless steel/gold-plated, automatic, ETA calibre 7751, full calendar, moon phase display and 24-hour display, from 1999

**Sinn**
Multifunction Chronograph, stainless steel, automatic, ETA calibre 7750, 24-hour display (dual time zone), from 2006

**Sinn**
Rallye Chronograph, stainless steel, automatic, ETA calibre 7750, with power reserve display, from 2006

## Fly-Back

Fly-Back is the name of another, unusual additional function that has led to renewed interest within the watch industry. The expression has little to do with flying, but relates to a mechanism whereby the chronograph can be switched back to zero without having to be stopped first.

To achieve this, the chronograph has to be designed in such a way that the reset-to-zero lever, activated by the lower pusher at four o'clock, which is normally blocked when the chronograph function is in operation, can also be moved when the chronograph is running.

When this happens, the lever flips against both heart pieces on the arbours of the chronograph centre wheel and the minutes counting wheel. This mighty blow causes the heart pieces to lie flat against the heart piece lever. When the pusher is released the heart piece lever jumps back and the chronograph immediately runs again.

## Countless variations

Describing the variety of wonderful watches classed as chronographs would go far beyond the space available in this book. It is hardly surprising that there are books that deal exclusively with this kind of watch. Their importance is shown by the fact that this

**Sothis**
Chronograph Spirit of Moon, stainless steel, automatic, ETA calibre 7751, full calendar, from 1999

**Sothis**
Janus, stainless steel, automatic,
ETA calibre 7750, from 2006

**Sothis**
Chronograph Big Bridge, stainless
steel, automatic, ETA calibre 2892-A2
with Dubois-Dépraz chronograph
module 2025, from 1999

**TAG Heuer**
S/el Chronograph, stainless steel,
automatic, ETA calibre 7750,
from 1999

**TAG Heuer**
6000 Chronometer Chronograph, stainless steel, automatic,
ETA calibre 2894-2, C.O.S.C. certified chronometer, from 1999

**TAG Heuer**
Monaco Re-Edition, stainless steel, automatic,
ETA calibre 2894-2, from 1999

**TAG Heuer**
Carrera Chronograph, stainless steel,
automatic, TAG Heuer calibre 16
(base calibre ETA 7750), from 2006

**TAG Heuer**
Microtimer, stainless steel, quartz, TAG
Heuer calibre HR 03, measuring accuracy
1/1000 seconds, from 2006

**TAG Heuer**
1964 Heuer Carrera Re-Edition,
stainless steel, manual wind,
Lémania calibre 1873, from 1999

**TAG Heuer**
Link Chronograph, stainless steel, automatic, TAG
Heuer calibre 16 (base calibre ETA 7750), from 2006

**TAG Heuer**
Monaco Chronograph Steve
McQueen, stainless steel, automatic,
TAG Heuer calibre 17 (base calibre
ETA 2894-2), from 2006

chapter takes up almost a fifth of the whole book. Even more so, in the light of the fact that several of the following chapters (aviator watches, divers' watches, calendar watches) are concerned with timepieces that can also be used for measuring short intervals of time.

What is particularly gratifying is that over the last few years several noteworthy new designs have joined the many ETA/Valjoux calibre 7750-based chronographs. Some designs use, amongst others, Zenith, Patek Philippe, Rolex, A. Lange & Söhne, Glashütte Original and Jaeger-LeCoultre movements. It is also interesting to note that several watch brands have recently modified the description 'chronograph' for their watches. With Glashütte Original's 'PanoRetroGraph' or A. Lange & Söhne's 'Dato-Graph', new words have been coined that are as unusual as the watches themselves that bear the names. To be honest, few chronograph wearers really need a watch like

**TAG Heuer**

Monza Chronograph, stainless steel, automatic, TAG Heuer calibre 17 (base calibre ETA 2894-2), from 2006

**Temption**

Chronograph, stainless steel, automatic, Temption calibre T17.1 (base calibre ETA 7750), from 1999

**Temption**

Complex Chronograph, stainless steel, automatic, Temption calibre 17.2 (base calibre ETA 7751), full calendar, 24-hour display, from 1999

**TAG Heuer**

Calibre 360, stainless steel, automatic/manual wind, TAG Heuer calibre 360, measuring accuracy 1/100 seconds, from 2006

**Temption**

Chronograph Formula, stainless steel, automatic, Temption calibre T17.1 (base calibre ETA 7750), from 2006

this. But they are simply nice toys with a distinctly masculine aura. And a man will always welcome more of those.

## Historical digression: What is time measurement, actually?

Of course, the question again arises as to how you actually set about measuring time; what is the exact definition of the word 'time' itself? Prosaic science teaches us that 'time is the sequence of events'. O.K., so how do you measure the interval from one 'event' to the next?

People have created arbitrary units for all possible measurements, be they of weight, air pressure, or temperature. Even the original metre, introduced in 1795 in France as a 40-millionth part of the length of a meridian, was, at the end of the day, arbitrarily determined – it would have been equally possible to define a meter as a 20-millionth part of the distance from the north to the south pole.

But we must remember that by plotting the course of the stars and the regular, constantly recurring celestial phenomena, nature provided us with ideal units for measuring time. For

### Temption

Cherubin-R Chronograph Rattrapante, stainless steel, automatic, Temption calibre 19.1 (base calibre ETA calibre 7750), split-second hand function, from 2006

### Tissot

Chronograph, stainless steel, manual wind with column wheel operation, from 1950

### Tissot

Chrono Valjoux, stainless steel, automatic, ETA calibre 7750, from 2006

### Tissot

PRS Chrono Valjoux, stainless steel, automatic, ETA calibre 7750, from 2006

### Tudor

Oyster Date Chronograph, stainless steel, manual wind, calibre Valjoux 234, from 1980

127

**Tudor**
Prince Date Chronograph, stainless steel, automatic, ETA calibre 7750-1, from 2006

**Tutima**
Chronograph F2 PR, stainless steel, automatic, ETA calibre 7750, with power reserve display, from 2006

**Ulysse Nardin**
Chronograph, yellow gold, manual wind, single pusher chronograph with column wheel, from 1925

example, the earth's rotation, the phases of the moon or the even rotation of the moon around the earth, the orbit of the sun and the regular appearance of the fixed stars in the night-time sky were the first observed and 'measured' periods of time.

Buildings from antiquity and structures that pre-date our written history bear witness to the extensive knowledge that our ancestors had already gleaned merely from observing the stars. These people were already aware of the return of particular constellations and even decided on specific details of buildings to make them into astronomical instruments. For example, the sun might only shine through a hole in the wall on to a particular point inside the building on the first day of spring and autumn.

Even the Catholic church, which had for a long time challenged the existence of our heliocentric planetary system and wasn't deemed particularly astronomy friendly, having only vindicated the great astronomer Galileo

**Ulysse Nardin**
Chronograph, yellow gold, manual wind, one-pusher chronograph with column wheel operation, enamel dial with double tachymeter scale, from 1930

**Ulysse Nardin**
Marine Chronograph, stainless steel, automatic, Ulysse Nardin calibre 36 (base calibre ETA 2892), from 1999

Right: Three fine chronographs from the traditional Swiss brands Omega, Eterna and IWC

**Ulysse Nardin**
Split-Second Chronograph Berlin I,
yellow gold, automatic, Ulysse Nardin
calibre UN 57, from 1999

**Union**
Tradition Automatic Chronograph,
stainless steel, automatic, Union
calibre 26-31, from 1999

**Union**
Sport Chronograph, stainless steel,
automatic, Union calibre 26-31, from 1999

**Union**
Diplomat Chronograph, stainless steel,
automatic, Union calibre 26-32, from 2006

Galilei towards the end of the twentieth century, has admitted that small holes used to be made in the roofs of some churches in Italy. Through these, on particular days of the year (for example, the equinox) a shaft of light fell on to a particular point on the church floor. Some of these light passages were even designed so that over the course of the year, the sunlight, which was concentrated into a point, formed an imaginary line of light on the floor of the church.

Of course, it was to be a long way from these astronomical observations to more accurate time measurement. Ultimately, it came about that the period of time between the highest point of the sun on two successive days was divided into two lots of 12, and the highest point of the sun became the middle of the day – the end of the first and the beginning of the second 12-hour period – i.e. 'midday'.

**Universal Genève**
Chronograph, red gold, manual wind, calibre 285 with column wheel operation, from 1950

**Union**
Tradition Chronograph, stainless steel, automatic, Union calibre 26-31, from 1999

**Universal Genève**
Golden Master Tech, yellow gold, manual wind, Universal Genève calibre 88 (base calibre ETA 7760), from 1999

**Universal Genève**
Golden Compax 1950, stainless steel, manual wind, Universal Genève calibre 84 (base calibre Lémania 1873), from 1999

**Universal Genève**
Senna Watch, stainless steel/carbon, manual wind, Universal Genève calibre 98 (base calibre ETA 7750), from 1999

131

## Urban Jürgensen & Sønner

Referenz 1, platinum, automatic, Zenith calibre 4001 El Primero, from 2006

## Vacheron Constantin

Les Historiques Chronograph, Vacheron Constantine calibre 1140, from 1999

## Vacheron Constantin

Royal Eagle Chronograph, rose gold, automatic, Vacheron Constantin calibre 1137, from 2006

## Vacheron Constantin

Chronograph, yellow gold, manual wind, calibre V434 with column wheel operation, from 1938

## Victorinox

AirBoss Mach 6, stainless steel, automatic, ETA calibre 7753, from 2006

**George J. von Burg**
Classic Collection, gold-plated steel,
automatic, ETA 7750, from 2006

**Louis Vuitton**
Speedy Chronograph Automatique,
steel, automatic, ETA calibre 2894-2,
from 2006

**Raymond Weil**
Parsifal Chronograph, steel/yellow-
gold, automatic, ETA calibre 2829-A2,
from 1999

The resulting hours – which the Catholic-influenced Romance languages called *hora*, *heures*, or *ora* after the prayer said at canonical hours, were in turn divided into 60 smaller periods of time, the minutes (from Latin *minuere*, meaning to diminish). The second subdivision of the hour (Latin *secunda*, meaning the second) into even smaller segments, introduced later, was in turn a sixtieth of the next largest unit (the minute), so stayed within the twelve-fold system and was – surprise – called the second.

In English this division of the day into two lots of 12 'hours' became particularly embedded in the language, because 'forenoon' (from 12:00 midnight) is generally denoted with 'ante meridian' (a.m., *ante* being the Latin for 'before'), and 'afternoon' (from midday to midnight) with 'post meridian' (p.m., *post* being the Latin for 'after'), which signifies nothing more than the climb of the sun to its highest point on the meridian as it stands vertical to the horizon, and its subsequent descent.

Because of the tilting of the earth's axis, this takes place in daylight periods of varying length in summer and winter, resulting in hours during the Middle Ages also being of an irregular length. This came to an end after the invention of the first gear clocks, because a clockwork movement runs down at an even rate

**Raymond Weil**
Parsifal Chronograph, stainless steel, automatic, RW calibre 7300 (base calibre ETA 2894-2), from 2006

**Raymond Weil**
Saxo Automatic Chronograph, stainless steel, automatic, ETA calibre 7750, from 1999

**Xemex**
Avenue Chronograph, stainless steel, automatic ETA 2894-2, from 2006

influenced to a limited extent by the regulation of an oscillating system (verge-and-foliot, balance, pendulum).

When the measurement of time wasn't taken quite so seriously, clocks only had one hand, for the hours. Accuracy of the measurement process, vaguely comparable to the precision of mechanical clocks by today's standards, was only reached towards the end of the seventeenth and during the eighteenth centuries.

**Zenith**
Grand ChronoMaster GT, stainless steel, automatic, Zenith calibre 4001 El Primero, from 2006

**Harry Winston**
Pulsometer Chronograph, platinum, automatic Frédéric Piguet calibre 1185, from 1999

**Zenith**
Class El Primero, stainless steel, automatic, Zenith calibre 4002 El Primero, from 2006

### Zenith

Chronomaster Chronograph,
stainless steel, automatic, Zenith
calibre 400 El Primero, C.O.S.C.
certified chronometer, from 1999

### Zenith

Class 4 Chronograph, stainless
steel, automatic, Zenith calibre 400
El Primero, from 1999

### Zenith

Chronograph, sterling silver, manual
wind, crown pusher chronograph with
column wheel operation, from 1920

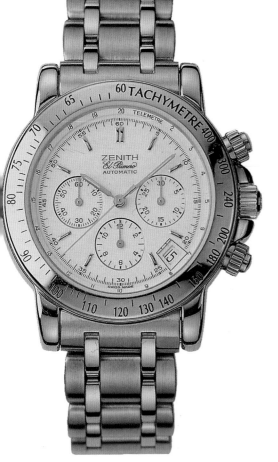

### Zenith

Port-Royal Open Concept, titanium,
automatic, Zenith calibre 4021 C El Primero,
works partly skeletized, from 2006

### Zenith

Rainbow Chronograph, steel, automatic, Zenith
calibre 400 El Primero, from 1999

### Zenith

Chronomaster Open XXT, stainless
steel, automatic, Zenith calibre 4021
El Primero, works partly skeletized,
from 2006

135

# 3. AVIATOR WATCHES

What *is* a proper aviator watch? This is a subject discussed by pilots as frequently, and often as hotly, as by watch manufacturers. The smallest common denominator is generally that an aviator watch must be a highly accurate timekeeper that can be read easily, even in unfavourable conditions. At the same time there is a whole range of features that are definitely as important in the cockpit as they are in everyday life.

**Aristo**
XL Edition Navigator, stainless steel, automatic, ETA calibre 2801, from 2006

**Bell & Ross**
Vintage 126 XL, stainless steel, automatic, ETA calibre 2894-2, chronograph, from 2006

**Bell & Ross**
Instrument BR01-94, stainless steel/black PVD-coated, automatic, ETA calibre 2894-2, chronograph, from 2006

The jewellery and watch manufacturer Cartier is not necessarily regarded as a sports watch specialist. And yet the first timepiece to have earned the designation 'aviator watch' came from this very company. During a dinner in Maxim's, Alberto Santos-Dumont, renowned in Parisian society as a dandy and an aviation pioneer during the Belle Époque, was explaining the big problem with his pocket watch. Because he had his hands literally full when carrying out his experiments with helium balloons, he simply wasn't able to monitor his flight times.

This was the era when pocket watches were carried on gold chains. To pull it out of his pocket, read it, and put it back in the pocket would have entailed an extremely dangerous loss of control over the aircraft. Louis-Joseph Cartier, a friend of Santos-Dumont, was listening attentively – and together with the watchmaker and master craftsman, Edmond Jaeger, he developed the first wristwatch. It had Roman numerals, two hands, a crown with a good grip, and was fastened to the wearer's wrist by means of a leather strap.

## Good legibility is the number one priority

This historical retrospective highlights features that are still important. These include first and

**Breitling**

Navitimer, stainless steel, manual wind, Venus calibre 178, chronograph, bidirectional rotating bezel with slide rule scale, from 1969

**Breguet**

Transatlantique, stainless steel, automatic, Breguet calibre 582Q, chronograph with Fly-Back function, bidirectional rotating bezel, from 1999

**Breitling**

Colt Ocean Automatic, stainless steel, automatic, Breitling calibre 17 (base calibre ETA 2892-2), unidirectional 60-minute bezel, from 1999

**Breguet**

Type XX Transatlantique, stainless steel, automatic, Breguet calibre 582Q, chronograph with Fly-Back function, bidirectional rotating bezel, from 2006

**Breitling**

Navitimer, stainless steel, automatic, calibre 12 with micro motor, chronograph, bidirectional rotating bezel with slide rule scale, from 1968

139

**Breitling**

Colt Superocean, yellow gold, automatic, Breitling calibre 10 (base calibre ETA 2892-2), C.O.S.C. certified chronometer, unidirectional 60-minute bezel, from 1969

**Breitling**

Montbrillant, stainless steel, automatic, Breitling calibre 19 (base calibre ETA 2892-A2), full calendar with moon phase display, bidirectional rotating bezel with slide rule scale, from 1999

**Breitling**

Spatiographe, stainless steel, automatic, Breitling calibre 36 (base calibre ETA 2892-A2), ten-minute digital totalizer at nine o'clock, bidirectional rotating bezel with slide rule scale, from 2006

**Breitling**

Navitimer Twinsixty, stainless steel, automatic, Breitling calibre 36 (base calibre ETA 2892-A2), bidirectional rotating bezel with slide rule scale, from 1999

**Breitling**

Navitimer Heritage, white gold, automatic, Breitling calibre 35 (base calibre ETA 2892-2), C.O.S.C. certified chronometer, bidirectional rotating bezel with slide rule scale, from 2006

**Breitling**

Emergency Mission, stainless steel, quartz, Breitling calibre 73 (base calibre ETA 251.262), C.O.S.C. certified chronometer, bidirectional 60-minute bezel, distress transmitter, from 2006

foremost secure attachment of the watch to the wrist, and in such a way that it can always be seen and read. Pilots in the First and Second World Wars sometimes had their watches fitted with extra-long leather straps that allowed the watch to be worn over a thick jacket or overalls – if necessary even on the thigh.

The second important feature of an aviator watch is its instant legibility. This is an area where, even in the digital age, an analogue watch scores over a digital. We westerners are so used to them that we are able to interpret the position of two hands in a fraction of a second, whilst a digital display has to be read properly. This is also an important consideration for the armed forces. Easy readability is the number one priority. It is for this reason that most modern timepieces that are designated 'aviator watches' have black dials with white numbers and hands, which also have a luminous coating and a specially marked 12 o'clock position for better night-time visibility. This was how the first 'Special Watch for Pilots' made by Swiss manufacturer IWC looked, which also featured

**Breitling**

Navitimer, stainless steel, automatic, Breitling calibre 23 (base calibre ETA 7750), C.O.S.C. certified chronometer, bidirectional rotating bezel with slide rule scale, from 2006

**Certina**

DS Pilot Automatic Chrono, stainless steel, automatic, Certina calibre 674 (base calibre ETA 7750), from 2006

### Cyma
Military watch, manual wind, stainless steel, British military wristwatch, from 1940

### Doxa
Flieger II, stainless steel, manual wind, ETA calibre 2801, from 2006

### Doxa
Aviator Chronograph, stainless steel, manual wind, German Luftwaffe military watch, from 1940

### Chronoswiss
Timemaster Fly-Back, stainless steel, automatic, Chronoswiss calibre C.673 (base calibre ETA 7750), chronograph with Fly-Back function, dial with luminescent coating, from 2006

### Doxa
Antimagnetic, stainless steel, manual wind, from 1940

**Enicar**
Jet Graph, stainless steel, manual
wind, calibre Valjoux 724, rotating
bezel for setting a second time zone,
from 1969

**Eterna**
Airforce III Chronograph, stainless
steel, automatic, ETA calibre 7750,
bidirectional 60-minute bezel,
from 1999

**Eterna**
Airforce II, stainless steel, automatic,
ETA calibre 2824-2, from 1999

**Eterna**
Aviator Watch, stainless steel,
manual wind, calibre 852S, German
Luftwaffe military watch, from 1935

143

**Excelsior Park**
Chronograph Monte Carlo, stainless
steel, manual wind, calibre Valjoux
7740, rotating 60-minute bezel,
from 1975

a rotating glass bezel with a luminous arrow
index.

A prime example as regards ease of legibility is
deemed to be the *Beobachtungsuhr* − or 'B-Uhr' for
short − used by German Luftwaffe pilots. They
were made in the 1940s by Wempe, Lange &
Söhne and IWC, as well as the Pforzheim brands
Stowa and Laco. Today the ranges of the last
three brands feature modern versions of their
earlier *Profiuhren*, which are very popular with
the public, mainly due to their functionality,
but also because of their history.

## Soft-iron inner cases give protection from magnetic fields

Strictly speaking, magnetic field protection for
the movement has been one of the key features
of a watch since the Second World War. The
screens of the ground-penetrating radars,

**Fortis**
Automatic Aviator Chronograph, stainless steel,
automatic, ETA calibre 7750, from 1999

**Fortis**
Pilot Professional Automatic,
steel/black PVD-coated, automatic,
ETA calibre 2836-2, from 1999

**Jacques Etoile**
Lissabon Grand Aviator, stainless
steel, manual wind, modified ETA
calibre Unitas, from 1999

**Fortis**
B-42 Official Cosmonauts'
Chronograph, stainless steel,
automatic ETA calibre 7750, special
edition with engraving on case back
(picture of ISS space station), limited
to 500 copies, from 2006

**Fortis**
Official Cosmonauts' Chronograph,
stainless steel, automatic, Lémania
calibre 5100, additional 24-hour
display (second time zone), from 1999

**Fortis**
Automatic Aviator, stainless steel,
automatic, ETA calibre 2824-2,
from 2006

**Glashütte Original**
Senator Aviator Automatic
Panorama Date, stainless steel,
automatic, Glashütte Original
calibre 39-42, from 1999

**Glashütter Uhrenbetrieb**
Tutima Chronograph, stainless steel,
manual wind, Urofa calibre 59 with
column wheel operation, known as
the Wehrmachtschronograph (army
chronograph), from 1942

**Glashütte Original**

Senator Aviator Automatic, stainless steel, automatic, Glashütte Original calibre 39-10, from 1999

**Glashütte Original**

Senator Aviator Chronograph, stainless steel, automatic, Glashütte Original calibre 39-30, from 1999

**Hamilton**

Aviator Watch, stainless steel, manual wind, calibre H75, British Royal Air Force military watch, from 1965

installed in increasing numbers, generated magnetic fields of such intensity that a watch's operation could be considerably influenced.

Nowadays alloys are used in the escapement mechanism, particularly for the hairspring, because they are less sensitive towards magnetism. However, magnetic fields in cockpits can still have a negative influence on a watch. Even today, aviator watch manufacturers – such as Sinn and IWC – who follow accepted wisdom continue to equip their timepieces with inner casings made from soft iron that leads the magnetic fields around the movement.

For pilots and 'seconds pinchers' amongst watch-lovers, a watch without a stop-seconds function is inconceivable. This is a mechanism that stops the watch when the crown is pulled out and starts it again when it is pushed in. This allows watches to be synchronized with each other or with an external radio signal, something that was particularly valuable when used by the military.

**Glycine**

Airman MLV, stainless steel, automatic, ETA calibre 2893-2, additional 24-hour display (second time zone), dial fully luminescent-coated, from 2006

## Hanhart

Tachy-Tele, stainless steel, manual wind, Hanhart calibre 40, German military chronograph with tachymetre and telemetre scales, from 1935

## Hanhart

One-Touch Aviator Chronograph, stainless steel, manual wind, Hanhart calibre 40, German Luftwaffe military watch, from 1935

## Hamilton

Military Watch, manual wind, calibre H75, British military watch, from 1973

## Hanhart

One-Touch Aviator Chronograph, stainless steel, manual wind, Hanhart calibre 40, bidirectional rotating bezel with reference mark, German Luftwaffe military watch, from 1936

## Hanhart

Aviator Chronograph, stainless steel, manual wind, Hanhart calibre 40, bidirectional rotating bezel with reference mark, German Luftwaffe military watch, from 1945

## Hamilton

Aviator Chronograph, stainless steel, manual wind, calibre Valjoux 7733, British Royal Air Force military watch, from 1969

147

**Heuer**

German Army Aviator Chronograph, stainless steel, manual wind, calibre Valjoux 233, chronograph with Fly-Back function, bidirectional rotating bezel with 0 to 60 markings, from 1970

**Heuer**

Aviator Chronograph, stainless steel, manual wind, calibre Valjoux 7733, chronograph with Fly-Back function, bidirectional rotating bezel with 0 to 12 markings, Argentine Air Force military watch, from 1975

**Hanhart**

Tachy-Tele Replica, stainless steel, manual wind, ETA calibre 7760, chronograph, bidirectional rotating bezel with reference markings, from 2006

**Hanhart**

Pioneer Calibre II, stainless steel, automatic, Hanhart calibre 716 (base calibre ETA 7750), chronograph, bidirectional rotating bezel with luminous mark, from 2006

**Hanhart**

Primus, stainless steel, manual wind, Hanhart calibre 704 (base calibre ETA 7760), single-pusher chronograph, bidirectional rotating bezel with reference markings, from 2006

**IWC**

Mark XI, stainless steel, automatic, IWC calibre 89, soft-iron inner case for protection against magnetic fields, British Royal Air Force military watch, from 1951

## Ikepod

Megapode Pilot Chronograph, stainless steel, automatic, ETA calibre 7750, C.O.S.C. certified chronometer, additional 24-hour display (second time zone), rotating bezel under glass with slide rule function, from 1999

**IWC**

Aviator Watch, stainless steel, manual wind, IWC calibre 52, German Luftwaffe military watch, from 1940

## IWC

Mark XII, stainless steel, automatic, IWC calibre C.884/2, soft-iron inner case for protection against magnetic fields, from 1999

**IWC**

Mark X, stainless steel, automatic, IWC calibre 83, soft-iron inner case for protection against magnetic fields, British Royal Air Force military watch, from 1944

149

## IWC

Mark XV, stainless steel, automatic, IWC calibre 37524 (base calibre ETA 2892-A2), soft-iron inner case for protection against magnetic fields, from 2006

## Robust construction is a necessity

Although it is generally dry in cockpits – the one exception being pre-war aircraft – even a pilot's watch comes into contact with water time and again both before and after the flight, making water-resistance another essential feature. But a word of caution: don't trust everything you read on a watch! A watch declared water-resistant to a depth of 30 metres (98 feet) in accordance with DIN specifications is not suitable for anything *less* than a dive to 30 metres. Watches like this are immune to spray, hand washing or a walk in the rain. But if you want to go for a swim with your watch, select one that is water-resistant to 100 metres (328 feet), according to DIN specifications.

**IWC**

UTC, stainless steel, automatic, IWC calibre C.37526, additional 24-hour display in dial window at 12 o'clock (second zone time), soft-iron inner case for protection against magnetic fields, from 1999

**IWC**

Aviator chronograph, stainless steel, automatic, IWC calibre C.7922 (base calibre ETA 7750), soft-iron inner case for protection against magnetic fields, from 1999

**IWC**

Aviator Watch Double Chronograph, stainless steel, automatic, IWC calibre 79230 (base calibre ETA 7750), chronograph with split-second hand, soft-iron inner case for protection against magnetic fields, from 1999

**IWC**

Large Aviator Watch, stainless steel, automatic, IWC calibre 5011, soft-iron inner case for protection against magnetic fields, from 2006

This IWC Double Chrono has classic aviator watch looks: clearly legible dial typography, additional functions and a case in non-reflective matt black

In a pilot's everyday life, the quality of the watch is also of paramount importance. So the Omega Speedmaster Professional, which acquired the name 'Moon Watch' after being used in various Apollo missions, was and still is fitted with a plastic crystal. Due to its resilience, it can equalize differences in pressure without jumping out or cracking, but it is susceptible to scratching; however, in contrast to mineral glass crystals, scratches can be polished out of Plexiglas. Nowadays, the first choice for quality watches is a sapphire crystal with a non-reflective coating on one side. These watch crystals are scratch-resistant and easy to read.

### IWC

Spitfire Double Chronograph, stainless steel, automatic, IWC calibre 79230 (base calibre ETA 7750), chronograph with split-second hand, soft-iron inner case for protection against magnetic fields, from 2006

### Daniel JeanRichard

Bressel Militaire, stainless steel, manual wind, calibre 16 DJR (base calibre ETA Unitas), from 1999

### Daniel JeanRichard

Automatic Militaire, stainless steel, automatic, calibre 24 DJR (base calibre ETA 2824-2), from 1999

### Jaeger-LeCoultre

LeCoultre Chronograph, stainless steel, manual wind, calibre Valjoux 72, bidirectional rotating bezel with 0 to 60 markings, from 1970

### Junghans

German Military Aviator Chronograph, stainless steel/chrome-plated, manual wind, Junghans calibre 88, German Luftwaffe military watch, from 1950

**Junghans**
Military Aviator Chronograph, stainless steel/chrome-plated, manual wind, Junghans calibre 88, bidirectional rotating bezel with 0 to 60 markings, German Luftwaffe military watch, from 1955

**Junghans**
Chronograph, stainless steel, manual wind, Junghans calibre 88, from 1945

## The watch as a navigational aid

An important function of the watch in the pioneer years of flying was navigation, particularly with long-distance flights. Pilots navigated in the same way as sailors and using the same aids, which included an accurately functioning watch. Charles A. Lindbergh wore a watch like this during his first Atlantic crossing. His annoyance over the shortcoming of this timepiece enriched the world of watches with another function: it enabled the geographical longitude to be calculated using degrees and minutes of arc.

Lindbergh's friendship with the President of the Fédération Aéronautique Internationale, John Heinmüller, whose main profession was Chairman of Longines Wittnauer Watch Co. in the USA, was instrumental in the creation of the

**Junghans**
Pilot Automatic, stainless steel, automatic, ETA calibre 2824-2, unidirectional rotating bezel with 0 to 60 markings, from 2006

**Laco**
Automatic Aviator Chronograph, stainless steel, automatic, ETA calibre 7750, from 2006

**Laco**
Series I Automatic Aviator Chronograph, stainless steel, automatic, ETA calibre 2824-2, from 2006

**A. Lange & Söhne**

B-Uhr Navigation Watch, silver, manual wind, Lange calibre with optimum timekeeping performance, degree measuring watch for the German Luftwaffe, only nine copies of this model were made, from 1939

**A. Lange & Söhne**

Aviator Watch, silver, manual wind, Lange calibre 45, German Luftwaffe military watch, from 1943

**Lémania**

Aviator Chronograph, stainless steel, manual wind, German Luftwaffe military watch, from 1938

155

**Lémania**
One-Touch Aviator Chronograph, stainless steel, manual wind, Lémania calibre 2220, Swedish Air Force military watch, from 1960

**Lémania**
Aviator Watch, stainless steel, manual wind, German Luftwaffe military watch, from 1935

**Lémania**
One-Touch Aviator Chronograph, stainless steel, manual wind, Lémania calibre 2220, British Royal Air Force military watch, from 1965

**Lémania**
One-Touch Aviator Chronograph, stainless steel, manual wind, Lémania calibre 2225, British Royal Air Force military watch, from 1950

**Longines**
Weems, stainless steel, manual wind, Longines calibre 12.68N, rotating bezel with 0 to 60 markings, British Royal Air Force navigation watch, from 1938

legendary 'Hour Angle Watch'. Based on Lindbergh's ideas and sketches, the timepiece was presented in 1931. It had a device for quick alignment of the seconds with a time signal – an inner dial that could be adjusted using the crown. The rotating bezel was divided into 15 degrees (with subdivisions into 15, 30 and 45 minutes of arc), as the earth turns by exactly 15 degrees in one hour (360 degrees in 24 hours = 15 degrees in one hour). Besides the 12-hour scale, the main dial was also subdivided into 180 degrees (corresponding to the earth's rotation in half a day). The rotating sub-dial was printed with 60-degree and 15-degree scales.

All of these scales and data necessitated a large dial so that it was still possible to see the big

**Longines**
Aviator Watch, stainless steel, manual wind, Longines calibre 15.94, German Luftwaffe military watch, from 1936

## Longines

Aviator Watch, stainless steel, manual wind, Longines calibre 330, rotating bezel with 0 to 12 markings, from 1968

## Longines

Aviator Watch, stainless steel, manual wind, Longines calibre 14.68N, British Air Force military watch, from 1951

## Longines

Lindbergh Hour Angle Watch, yellow gold, automatic, Longines calibre L.614.2 (base calibre ETA 2892-A2), bidirectional rotating bezel for calculating longitude, replica of historic Lindbergh watch, from 1999

## Longines

Lindbergh Hour Angle Watch, stainless steel, manual wind, Longines calibre 18.69N, bidirectional rotating bezel for calculating longitude, from 1936

## Marcello C.

Aviator Chronograph, stainless steel, automatic, ETA calibre 7750, from 1999

**Minerva**
Aviator Chronograph, stainless steel,
manual wind, German Luftwaffe
military watch, with tachymetre scale,
from 1940

**Marcello C.**
Automatic Aviator, stainless steel,
automatic, ETA calibre 2824-2, from 1999

**Minerva**
Palladio S Aviation, stainless steel,
automatic, ETA calibre 7750, from 1999

**Minerva**
Aviator Chronograph, stainless steel,
manual wind, single button
chronograph, from 1930

**Minerva**
Pythagore Aviation, stainless
steel, automatic, Minerva
calibre 48, from 1999

## Mühle Glashütte

Marine Aviation Chronograph III, stainless steel, automatic, ETA calibre 7750, bidirectional rotating bezel with 0 to 60 markings, from 1999

## Mühle Glashütte

Marine Aviation Chronometer M2, stainless steel, automatic, ETA calibre 2824-2, C.O.S.C. certified chronometer, from 1999

## Nivada

Aviator Sea Diver, stainless steel, manual wind, calibre Landeron 248, rotating bezel, from 1969

## Mühle Glashütte

Lufthansa Tachymetre, stainless steel, automatic, ETA calibre 7750, bidirectional rotating inner bezel with 0 to 60 markings, from 2006

## Mühle Glashütte

Big Sports M12, stainless steel, automatic, ETA calibre 2824-2, from 2006

## Nivrel

Automatic Day Date, stainless steel, automatic, ETA calibre 2836-2, from 1999

**N. B. Yaeger**
Tango, stainless steel, automatic, ETA calibre 2893-2, additional 24-hour display (second time zone), from 2006

**N. B. Yaeger**
Delta, stainless steel, automatic, ETA calibre 2824-2, from 2006

**N. B. Yaeger**
Charlie, stainless steel, automatic, ETA calibre 7750, from 2006

**Omega**
Air Ministry Aviator Watch, stainless steel, manual wind, Omega calibre 23.4SC, rotating bezel with Weems seconds-setting, British Royal Air Force navigation watch, from 1940

**Omega**
Speedmaster Professional, stainless steel, manual wind, Omega calibre 321, chronograph, from 1963

**Omega**
Aviator Watch, stainless steel, manual wind, Omega calibre 283, soft-iron inner case for protection against magnetic fields, British Royal Air Force military watch, from 1953

picture when faced with this wealth of information. So the finished watch measured 47.5 millimetres (1.9 inches) in diameter. If the time signal was correctly set, the information in the Nautical Almanac taken into consideration, and the sextant used to calculate the degrees of latitude, it really was possible to read off the degree of longitude of one's actual position. Of course, nowadays, in our age of radar, GPS, and radio systems, something that was crucially important to Lindbergh and his contemporaries is just history and no longer particularly relevant. Today's pilots have completely different requirements from their watches.

## Oris

Flight Timer, stainless steel, automatic, ETA calibre with second zone time (at three o'clock), inner rotating bezel operated by separate crown at two o'clock (third zone time), from 2006

### Perrelet

Air Zermatt II, stainless steel, automatic, ETA calibre 2892-A2, inner rotating bezel with 0 to 60 markings, operated with additional crown at two o'clock, from 1999

## Omega

Flightmaster, stainless steel, manual wind, Omega calibre 911, chronograph, second zone time display, inner rotating bezel (Réhau) with 60-minute scale, from 1963

## Omega

Speedmaster Moonwatch Replica, stainless steel, manual wind, Omega calibre 1861 (base calibre Lémania 1873), chronograph, from 1999

### Poljot

JAK-7, stainless steel, manual wind, Poljot calibre 3133, chronograph, from 2006

### Record

Aviator Watch, stainless steel, manual wind, calibre 022K, British military watch, from 1948

### Revue Thommen

Airspeed Chronograph II, stainless steel, automatic, ETA calibre 7750, rotating bezel with 60-minute scale, from 1999

### Revue Thommen

Airspeed Automatic, stainless steel, automatic, ETA calibre 2836-2, from 1999

### Revue Thommen

Airspeed Altimetre, titanium, manual wind, ETA calibre 7001, mechanical altimetre, from 1999

### Revue Thommen

Airspeed Fly-Back, stainless steel, automatic, LIP calibre 8151 (base calibre ETA 7750), chronograph with Fly-Back function, from 2006

## Chronographs are in great demand from modern pilots

One of the most popular features at the moment is the chronograph stop function for measuring short intervals of time up to 12 hours. Porsche Design's 'Indicator' has assumed a special position amongst modern aviator chronographs. It is the only chronograph that displays stop minutes and hours in digital readout – purely mechanically, of course.

Advanced aviator watch fans tend to choose rattrapante chronographs with two timing hands. One hand is stopped to determine an intermediate or reference time, whilst the other hand continues to sweep round, hence the description 'split second'. If the reference time is no longer required, just one push on the button and the split-second hand jumps to rejoin the regular timing hand. So it catches it up, hence the description 'rattrapante', from

**Otto Schlund**
Korona Sport Aviator, stainless steel, automatic, ETA calibre 2824-2, from 2006

**Sinn**
Aviator Chronograph, stainless steel, automatic, ETA calibre 7750, chronograph, from 2006

**Sinn**
Aviator Chronograph, stainless steel, automatic, Lémania calibre 5100, stop-second and central minute timer, 24-hour display, from 1999

**Sinn**
Aviator Chronograph, stainless steel, automatic, Lémania calibre 5100, stop-second and central minute timer, 24-hour display, from 1999

**Sinn**
Space Chronograph, stainless steel, automatic, Lémania calibre 5100, stop-second and central minute timer, 24-hour display, from 1999

**Sinn**
Aviator with magnetic field protection, stainless steel, automatic, ETA calibre 2824-2, soft-iron inner case for protection against magnetic fields, from 2006

## Sinn

Aviator Watch with captive bezel, stainless steel, automatic, ETA calibre 2824-2, soft-iron inner case for protection against magnetic fields, from 2006

## TAG Heuer

Autavia, stainless steel, automatic TAG Heuer calibre 11 (base calibre Dubois-Dépraz 2022), from 2006

## Stowa

Aviator, stainless steel, automatic, ETA calibre 2824, extra long leather strap, from 2006

## Tissot

T-Touch Tech, stainless steel, quartz, ETA calibre E40.305, multifunctional electronics module with altimetre, chronograph etc. operated by touch-sensitive sensors in the crystal, from 2006

## Tutima

Aviator chronograph 1941, stainless steel, manual wind, ETA calibre 7760, bidirectional rotating bezel with reference marking, from 1999

## Tudor

Oyster Prince Ranger, stainless steel, automatic, from 1975

## Tutima

Military Aviator Chronograph T, titanium, automatic, Lémania calibre 5100, stop-second and central minute timer, 24-hour display, from 1999

## Tutima

Pacific, stainless steel, automatic, ETA calibre 2836-2, bidirectional rotating bezel with 60-minute scale, from 1999

## Tutima

Aviator Chronograph F2, stainless steel, automatic, ETA calibre 7750, bidirectional rotating bezel with reference marking, from 1999

**Tutima**
Automatic FX, stainless steel, automatic, ETA calibre 2836-2, bezel with 60-minute scale, from 2006

**Ulysse Nardin**
Aviator Chronograph A.R.A. Navigacion, silver, manual wind, crown pusher chronograph, from 1925

**Tutima**
Classic Aviator Chronograph, stainless steel, manual wind, ETA calibre 7760, bezel with reference marking, from 2006

**Tutima**
Military Aviator Chronograph II, stainless steel, automatic, Lémania calibre 5100, stop-second and central minute timer, 24-hour display, bezel with 60-minute sca from 2006

the French *rattraper*, meaning to catch up (see 'Chronograph' chapter). The Fly-Back function is also popular with many pilots. This enables the chronograph to be reset to zero and to continue running without pressing the start/stop button. So with just one push of a button a new measurement can be started. Incidentally the only chronograph to combine the rattrapante, Fly-Back and automatic movement is the Blancpain Léman Fly-Back Split-Second.

Frequent fliers, particularly those who move between different time zones, tend to choose watches which can display at least two times at once (e.g. the time at home and local time, or Zulu and local time). However, we have devoted the chapter 'GMT and World Time Watches'

**Union**
Aviator Chronograph,
stainless steel, automatic
Union calibre 26-32,
from 2006

**Union**
Aviator Small Second, stainless steel,
automatic Union calibre 26-05,
from 2006

**Universal Genève**
Rattrapante Aviator Chronograph,
steel, manual wind, 24-hour dial,
from 1940

**Zenith**
Aviator Chronograph, steel, automatic, Zenith calibre 146 DP, rotating bezel with 60-minute scale, from 1970

**Zenith**
Aviator Chronograph, steel, automatic, Zenith calibre 3091PHC, rotating bezel with 60-minute scale, approximately 2,700 examples of this watch were made, from 1972

**Victorinox**
AirBoss Mach 4 XL de Luxe, steel, manual wind, ETA calibre 6498-2, inner bezel with 60-minute scale, from 2006

**Zenith**
Rainbow Chronograph Fly-Back, steel, automatic, Zenith calibre 400 El Primero, from 1999

to these watches, where there is also an explanation of the technical function of this kind of watch.

Whilst the wristwatch was an essential piece of aircraft equipment in the early days of aviation, today it generally has a completely different function. Sergio de Witt, Lufthansa captain on an MD-11 Freighter, philosophized: 'The more digitized and highly technical our environment becomes, the greater the wish will be for something tangible and down to earth, that is embodied in a mechanical watch. It represents a likeable contrast to our fully electronic working environment. That is where I think their charm lies'.

The models for today's aviator watches originated during the Second World War and were primarily designed for optimum ease of use. Pictured to the right are two historic IWC watches from the 1940s.

# 4. DIVERS' WATCHES

Diving as a sport did not become really popular until about 25 years ago. Divers' watches, however, have been around for over 70 years. Books could be written about the development of divers' watches, chronographs and alarms. We are going to devote at least a chapter to the topic, turning the spotlight to illuminate individual episodes in the history of the divers' watch.

**Bertolucci**

Vir Maris men's divers' watch, steel, automatic, ETA calibre 2892-A2, C.O.S.C. certified chronometer, water-resistant to 300 m (985 ft), unidirectional rotating divers' bezel, from 1999

**Blancpain**

Fifty Fathoms divers' watch and divers' chronograph, steel, automatic, Blancpain calibre, water-resistant to 300 m (985 ft), unidirectional rotating divers' bezel, from the 1950s

**Blancpain**

Fifty Fathoms, steel, automatic, Blancpain calibre 1151, two spring barrels, water-resistant to 300 m (985 ft), unidirectional rotating divers' bezel, from 2006

The year 1927 probably counts as the year of birth of the water-resistant wristwatch. The young sportswoman Mercedes Gleitze swam the English Channel from Calais to Dover, with a Rolex on her wrist. Its case structure was patented, and among its distinguishing features was a back with a screw thread that allowed itself to be screwed into the case, plus a screw-threaded crown. The whole was supposed to be as watertight as an oyster, and so it was given its name. The Channel crossing offered the first public demonstration of this feature, and it made the papers on 24 November of that year. 'Rolex Oyster, the wonder watch that defies the elements' was the headline on the front page of the *Daily Mail*. This did not happen quite by chance, as Hans Wilsdorf, the owner of Rolex, had bought the front page of the newspaper, which had circulation figures in the millions, for 40,000 Swiss francs.

**Blancpain**

Air Command Concept, steel/rubber, automatic, Blancpain calibre F185, chronograph, water-resistant 200 m (657 ft), unidirection rotating divers' bezel, from 2

**Certina**
DS-3 Super PH 1000 m, steel, automatic, calibre 919-1, unidirectional rotating divers' bezel, water-resistant to 1000 m (3280 ft), from 1975

**Breitling**
Chrono Superocean, steel, automatic, Breitling calibre 13 (base ETA 7750), chronograph, C.O.S.C. certified chronometer, water-resistant to 500 m (1640 ft), unidirectional rotating divers' bezel, from 2006

**Bvlgari**
Scuba Chrono, steel, automatic, GP calibre 2282, chronograph, C.O.S.C. certified chronometer, water-resistant to 200 m (657 ft), unidirectional rotating divers' bezel, from 1999

**Certina**
DS-2, steel, automatic, calibre 25-651, unidirectional rotating divers' bezel, water-resistant to 100 m (328 ft), from 1968

This headline made the brand famous overnight, and ever since then it has been the name synonymous with a sturdy sports watch. Rolex did not become a divers' watch until much later. The Oyster case was systematically improved and was the foundation for the first Submariner, which came onto the market in 1953 and was water-resistant to a depth of 100 metres (328 feet). Only a year later, the water resistance was doubled to 200 metres (657 feet). A not inconsiderable contribution to this development came from two Swiss researchers, Auguste and Jacques Piccard, who went on their expeditions equipped with Rolex watches and gave the manufacturer's research and development staff many useful tips. Jacques Piccard made a spectacular advertisement for Rolex in 1960 by taking an Oyster on his dive into the Mariana Trench. He did not, however, wear it on his wrist. The timepiece was a special design called the Deep Sea

Special Oyster, fixed to the outer shell of the submarine *Trieste*. The timepiece, with its hefty case and hemispherical glass, withstood water pressure of more than one tonne per square centimetre at 10,916 metres (six tons per square inch at 38,815 feet) and remained absolutely watertight. The mass-produced mechanism fulfilled its task with no problems at all.

Rolex underwater timepieces were around well before Rolex divers' watches. In 1936 the Italian company Guido Panerai & Figlio, which later became Officine Panerai, designed the first prototype of a divers' watch. The client was the Italian navy, which had previously tested various Swiss watches but had not been satisfied. Now it was the turn of the Florentine company, specializing in fine mechanisms, which had also made mechanical depth gauges, compasses and torpedo detonators for the navy.

Panerai built a Rolex calibre into the case of a modified depth meter and delivered it in the same year to the Admiralty, which then ordered ten of them. The delivery of these watches in 1938 made Panerai the official watch supplier to the Italian navy.

The dial was a special feature. It was distinguished by optimum legibility, even in total darkness, and was comprised of two parts. The upper part was a black disc, with large figures and indexes punched out of it, and the lower part was a dial completely covered with luminous coating. The high radiance – or radiation – of the dial and the hands was due to a special mixture that included zinc sulphate and radium bromide.

The latter also helped give the watch its name of Radiomir and subjected its wearer to a strong dose of radioactivity. As if these soldiers were not in enough danger already!

### Ebel

Sportwave Diver, steel, Ebel calibre 120 (base ETA 2892-A2), water-resistant to 200 m (657 ft), unidirectional rotating divers' bezel, from 2006

### Chopard

L.U.C. Pro One, steel, automatic, L.U.C. calibre 4/96, C.O.S.C. certified chronometer, water-resistant to 300 m (985 ft), unidirectional rotating divers' bezel, from 2006

### Ebel

Discovery, steel, automatic, Ebel calibre 080 (based on Lémania 8815), water-resistant to 200 m (657 ft), unidirectional rotating divers' bezel, from 1999

### Doxa

Sub 750 T Professional, steel, automatic, ETA calibre 28245-2, water-resistant to 750 m (2460 ft), unidirectional rotating divers' bezel with decompression table, from 2006

### Doxa

Sub 600 T-Graph, steel, automatic, ETA calibre 2894-2, chronograph, water-resistant to 600 m (1970 ft), unidirectional rotating divers' bezel with decompression table, from 2006

These servicemen were part of a kind of swimmers' combat unit within the Italian navy. Two frogmen rode a steerable torpedo, a kind of underwater motorbike, in order to creep into Allied harbours and destroy enemy shipping with explosives. These special watch-equipped divers had their most spectacular mission in 1941, when they sank three important British navy ships in the harbour of Alexandria. In 1943, the Florentine watchmakers designed a chronograph intended for navy officers. This watch was known as Mare Nostrum, the ancient Romans' term for the Mediterranean. However, because of the Second World War, this project never got past the prototype stage.

In the early 1950s, Panerai delivered the Luminor model to the army, the later replacement for the Radiomir. The shape of the case and the design of the dial remained the same. The gamma ray-emitting radium, however, was replaced by the less dangerous

**Eterna**
Porsche Design titanium divers' watch, titanium, automatic, EternaMatic calibre 633 (base ETA 2824-2), water-resistant to 300 m (985 ft), unidirectional rotating divers' bezel, from 1999

**Enicar**
Super Dive Sherpa, steel, automatic, calibre AR 1145, unidirectional rotating inner divers' bezel, water-resistant to 100 m (328 ft), from 1970

**Eterna**
KonTiki Diver, steel, automatic, ETA calibre 2892-A2, water-resistant to 100 m (328 ft), unidirectional rotating inner divers' bezel, from 2006

**Jacques Etoile**
Atlantis, steel, automatic, ETA calibre 2824-2, water-resistant to 500 m (1640 ft), movement magnetic field protected, unidirectional rotating divers' bezel, from 2006

**Fortis**
Official Cosmonauts' Sports Diver, steel, automatic, ETA calibre 2836-2, water-resistant to 200 m (657 ft), unidirectional rotating divers' bezel, from 1999

tritium. The water resistance was also considerably improved, which was due not least to the very specialized crown seal, typical to this day of a Panerai Luminor. This was a crescent-shaped protective cover over the crown, with a little inbuilt lever. In order to set or wind the watch, the lever had to be released. When closed, it compressed the crown seal so much that no water could force its way in and the crown became immovable.

Military requirements continued to characterize the development of the divers' watch. In the 1950s, Captain Robert Maloubier was commissioned by the French Ministry of Defence to set up a new diving combat unit, the Nageurs du Combat. For this purpose, he had to find not only the right people, but also the right equipment. An extremely sturdy divers' watch, for example, reliable and precise at depths of almost 100 meters (330 feet). Interestingly, his divers' watch project ended

**Hublot**
Professional, steel/yellow gold, automatic, ETA calibre 2892-2, water-resistant to 300 m (985 ft), from 1999

**Fortis**
B-42 Diver Day Date, steel, automatic, ETA calibre 2836-2, water-resistant to 200 m (657 ft), unidirectional rotating divers' bezel, from 2006

**Girard-Perregaux**
Sea Hawk II Pro, titanium, automatic, GFP calibre 033R0 (based on GP 3300), movement magnetic field protection, water-resistant to 3000 m (9850 ft), power reserve indicator, case with two helium valves, from 2006

**Glashütte Original**
Sport Evolution, steel, automatic, Glashütte Original calibre 10-30, water-resistant to 200 m (657 ft), from 1999

### Glycine

Lagunare LCC 1000, steel, automatic, ETA calibre 2824-2, water-resistant to 300 m (985 ft), C.O.S.C. certified chronometer, unidirectional rotating divers' bezel, from 2006

### IWC

ATM Aquatimer, steel, automatic, IWC calibre 8541B, water-resistant to 300 m (985 ft), unidirectional rotating inner divers' bezel, from 2006

### IWC

Aquatimer Automatic 2000, titanium, automatic, IWC calibre 30110 (base ETA 2892-A2), water-resistant to 2000 m (6560 ft), unidirectional rotating divers' bezel, from 2006

### IWC

GST Aquatimer, titanium, automatic, IWC calibre C37524 (base ETA 2892-A2), water-resistant to 2000 m (6560 ft), unidirectional rotating divers' bezel, from 2006

### IWC

Aquatimer Split Minute Chronograph, titanium, automatic, IWC calibre 79740 (base ETA 7750), water-resistant to 120 m (394 ft), chronograph with split minute hand, unidirectional rotating inner divers' bezel, from 2006

### IWC

Aquatimer Automatic, steel, automatic, IWC calibre 30110 (base ETA 2892-A2), water-resistant to 1000 m (3280 ft), unidirectional rotating inner divers' bezel, from 2006

177

**Jaeger-LeCoultre**
Memovox Polaris, steel, automatic, calibre 425, unidirectional rotating inner divers' bezel, alarm function, water-resistant to 300 m (985 ft), from 1966

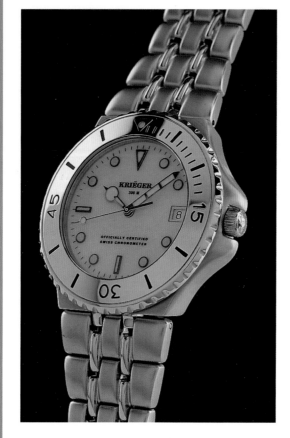

up in the Swiss Jura, with the clockmakers Blancpain, who developed a timepiece known as 'Fifty Fathoms', after the depth required.

A fathom, the traditional depth measurement of western navigation, is equivalent to 1.8 metres (6 feet). Maloubier therefore demanded guaranteed water resistance to a diving depth of 91 metres (300 feet), plus extremely good readability and a diving time bezel that could be used to determine diving and decompression times more exactly to within five minutes, that is to say an instrument important for the divers' safety, that could be used to apportion the limited supplies of breathable air in the divers' flasks. For this reason, too, Maloubier demanded that the bezel could only be moved anticlockwise.

**Krieger**
Hammerhead Pro Divers' Chronometer, steel, automatic, C.O.S.C. certified chronometer, water-resistant to 300 m (985 ft), from 1999

**Limes**
Endurance 1000, steel, automatic, ETA calibre 2824, water-resistant to 1000 m (3280 ft), unidirectional rotating divers' bezel, from 2006

**Longines**
Automatic Divers' Watch, steel, automatic, calibre 431, unidirectional rotating inner divers' bezel, from 1965

**Longines**
Automatic Divers' Watch, steel, automatic, calibre 290, unidirectional rotating inner divers' bezel, from 1965

therefore, if the bezel were accidentally moved, this would then lead to apparent increase in the time spent on the dive and to n earlier rising than scheduled.

Maloubier's specifications also demanded good legibility and Blancpain put this into practice with large numbers and hands coated with tritium. The watch passed its test on 0 November 1953 with flying colours. The French captain certified the excellence of he Swiss clockmakers' work with a plain *Bon*. The reliability, workmanship, precision, and ase of use of the 'Fifty Fathoms' became widely known, so that the elite US Navy Seals unit and the newly formed German military frogmen's unit decided in favour of Blancpain.

This watch was in official use with the German Bundeswehr until 1994. Then it was superseded by the Ocean, commissioned from IWC by the German military. The watchmakers from Schaffhausen in Germany won an official tender and in the spring of 1980 they received a

30-page set of specifications. This set out requirements such as precision, shock-proof qualities, temperature characteristics, thickness, and amagnetic characteristics. The last turned out to be a true challenge, as Jürgen King, then technical director of IWC, recalls: 'We had some experience with military watches, but neither we nor any other company had ever made amagnetic watches'. The background to this demand was that the detonators of certain mines react not only to pressure or sound, but also to the weakest of magnetic fields, such as may be caused by the movements of quartz watches. This meant that this new development must neither create nor change magnetic fields. Even the experienced Schaffhausen watchmakers had to do some basic research here, and work in unconventional ways. Because buildings are, for the most part, not free of disruptive magnetic fields, King took the test candidates and their equipment into his own garden and carried out measurements there. IWC was supported in its development and materials research by scientists at the

**Marcello C.**
Tridente Chronograph, steel, automatic, ETA calibre 7750, water-resistant to 300 m (985 ft), unidirectional rotating divers' bezel, from 2006

**Marcello C.**
Nettuno Chronograph steel, automatic, ETA calibre 7750, water-resistant to 300 m (985 ft), unidirectional rotating divers' bezel, from 2006

**Marcello C.**
Nettuno, steel, automatic, ETA calibre 2824-2, water-resistant to 200 m (657 ft), unidirectional rotating divers' bezel, from 1999

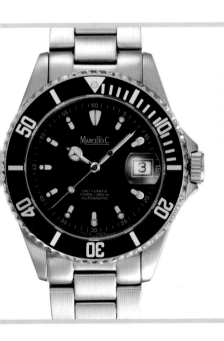

**Marcello C.**
Nettuno 3, steel, automatic, ETA calibre 2824-2, water-resistant to 300 m (985 ft), unidirectional rotating divers' bezel, from 2006

179

**Mido**

Ocean Star Sport Diver, steel, automatic, ETA calibre 2836-2, water-resistant to 200 m (657 ft), unidirectional rotating divers' bezel, from 2006

**Mido**

All Dial Diver, steel, automatic, ETA calibre 2836-2, water-resistant to 200 m (657 ft), unidirectional rotating inner divers' bezel, from 2006

**Nivada**

Depthomatic, steel, automatic, ETA calibre 2472, water-resistant to 200 m (657 ft), integrated mechanical depth gauge, unidirectional rotating divers' bezel, from 2006

**Mühle Glashütte**

Nautic-Timer, steel, automatic, ETA calibre 2824-2, water-resistant to 2000 m (6560 ft), unidirectional rotating divers' bezel, from 2006

University of Lausanne. The automatic works were to function like any other automatic works, only with tried and tested parts being replaced by amagnetic ones. This included the balance spring, made from a special alloy (niobium-zirconium). There is no further information officially available, because the amagnetic mine divers' watch is, just like the ordinary divers' automatic watch and the frogmen's watch with quartz movement, part of the navy's current equipment, and as such is issued a NATO supply number and comes under secrecy regulations.

King is, however, able to say this much: 'We were required to make a very hard-wearing watch. But until we got there, there was a lot of waste metal'. The requirement for a robust case and glass led to a seal tighter than any that had been attained up to that point. The Ocean

could withstand up to 200 bar (units o atmosphere pressure), corresponding to a depth of 2000 metres (6560 feet). The civilian version of the Ocean, designed, as the military watches were, by Ferdinand Alexander Porsche, was also given 2000 as an addition to its name, for the same reason.

When the Blancpain was becoming a little elderly, but the IWC was not yet finished, many navy frogmen decided on the first watch actually designed for sporting divers: the Doxa Sub 300. The unmissable feature of a Doxa divers' watch was and still is the orange dial. The spiritual father of this dial is considered to be Urs Eschle, Doxa's chief research and development man at the time. He dived in Lake Neufchatel with four plaques in different colours (turquoise, yellow, red, orange) and, based on the best legibility at

## Omega

Seamaster Automatic 600 m Ploprof, steel monocoque, automatic, Omega calibre, water-resistant to 600 m (1970 ft), unidirectional rotating divers' bezel, made for professional divers (hence the name Plongeurs Professionels – Ploprof), from 1972

## Omega

Seamaster Planet Ocean Co-Axial, steel, automatic, Omega calibre 2500C (based on Omega 1120), water-resistant to 600 m (1970 ft), unidirectional rotating divers' bezel, case with helium valve, from 2006

## Omega

Seamaster 300, steel, automatic, Omega calibre 565, water-resistant to 300 m (985 ft), unidirectional rotating divers' bezel, from 1969

## Omega

Seamaster Chrono Diver 300 m, steel, automatic, Omega calibre 3301, chronograph, C.O.S.C. certified chronometer, water-resistant to 300 m (985 ft), unidirectional rotating divers' bezel, case with helium valve, from 2006

## Omega

Seamaster Professional Diver, steel, automatic, Omega calibre 1120, C.O.S.C. certified chronometer, water-resistant to 300 m (985 ft), unidirectional rotating divers' bezel, from 1999

great depth, decided on orange, the colour of the 1970s. As a special feature, the designers equipped the bezel not just with a minutes ring, but also with a decompression table.

Alongside the total dive time, decompression is the most important time information for a diver. The extreme diver and scientist, Hannes Keller, was of the same opinion and, together with the researchers of the clockmakers Vulcain, he designed a new divers' watch. The Cricket Nautical was the first divers' alarm with integral decompression calculator, which had an acoustic alarm that would function even underwater. This alarm was to signal the preset time for surfacing.

Keller had big plans, as he wrote in a letter dated 3 July, 1961 to the Vulcain management: 'I am happy to be able to report that I have succeeded in setting a new world record in diving in Brissago on the afternoon of 28 June, 1961'. With his diving partner Kenneth McLeish, science editor for the American magazine, *Life*, Keller dived 222 metres (728 feet) down into Lago Maggiore, both wearing Cricket Nauticals on their wrists. In a letter, Keller is full of praise for the timepieces, which were subjected to 'extraordinary stresses' such as high temperatures and differences in pressure. 'Both watches performed excellently in the trials. I also tested the alarm mechanism of one of the two watches. The sound could be clearly heard,

**Oris**

TT1 Master Diver, titanium, automatic, Oris calibre 649 (base ETA 2836-2), regulator display, water resistant to 1000 m (3280 ft), unidirectional rotating divers' bezel, case with helium valve, from 2006

**Oris**

TT1 Divers Titanium, titanium, automatic, Oris calibre 633 (base ETA 2824-2), water resistant to 1000 m (3280 ft), unidirectional rotating divers' bezel, case with helium valve, from 2006

**Oris**

TT1 Divers Titanium Chronograph, titanium, automatic, Oris calibre 674 (base ETA 7750), water-resistant to 300 m (985 ft), unidirectional rotating divers' bezel, case with helium valve, from 2006

**Oris**

TT1 Divers Titanium Date, titanium, Oris calibre 633 (base ETA 2824-2), dial completely covered with luminous coating, water-resistant to 300 m (985 ft), unidirectional rotating divers' bezel, case with helium valve, from 2006

## Panerai

Luminor Submersible 2500, titanium, automatic, Panerai calibre OP III, C.O.S.C. certified chronometer, water-resistant to 1000 m (3280 ft), unidirectional rotating divers' bezel, from 2006

## Panerai

Radiomir Brevattato, steel, hand winding, frogmen's watch from the Italian navy, from 1938

## Panerai

Luminor Egittica, steel, hand winding, Angelus eight-day movement, frogmen's watch for the Egyptian navy, some 50 of these were made, from approximately 1956

Three chunky models from the early days of divers' watches

**Paul Picot**

Le Plongeur C-Type Date, steel, automatic, ETA calibre 2824-2, C.O.S.C. certified chronometer, water-resistant to 300 m (985 ft), unidirectional rotating divers' bezel, from 2006

**Poljot**

Red October, steel, automatic, Vostok calibre 2416.B, water-resistant to 300 m (985 ft), unidirectional rotating divers' bezel, from 2006

**Paul Picot**

Le Plongeur C-Type Chronograph, steel, automatic, ETA calibre 7752, C.O.S.C. certified chronometer, water resistant to 300 m (985 ft), unidirectional rotating divers' bezel, from 2006

even though my diving suit was fully closed..'. Legibility of the dial and the decompression table also met with Keller's full satisfaction, leading him to the following conclusion: 'With regard to this extraordinary performance, I have no doubt that the Vulcain Cricket Nautical Divers' Watch will be a great success on the market and that the watch will provide many divers with the same inestimable service that it has given us during these difficult tests'.

It was not to be the last time that an extreme diver cooperated in the development of a

divers' watch. On 6 July 1999, Mario Weidner set a record in the Arctic Sea. Weidner, who comes from Frankfurt am Main in Germany, achieved a dive to a depth of 64.5 metres (212 feet) in the ice-cold waters of the 81st parallel. Over his thick suit, he wore a watch that also came from Frankfurt, the Sinn Chronograph 203. The professional diver later commented for the record: 'The good legibility of the blue dial in combination with the slightly domed sapphire crystal, especially under water, was a particularly positive feature'. Sinn technicians who had accompanied the diver on his journey also noted that for the first time in practical application a special oil performed exactly as promised. Despite the great cold, the running of the automatic movement never diverged from its target values. And the case did not allow a single drop of Arctic water to penetrate. This meant that the Model 203 deserved the official addition 'Arktis' to its name.

An unofficial nickname, though one well-known even among non-divers, was given to a very popular divers' watch. The Omega Seamaster Professional is known in many quarters simply as the Bond watch, because it had to survive many difficult challenges on the wrist of Agent 007. The Seamaster made its first appearance in a Bond film in *Goldeneye* in 1995, where it had two clever details built into its case: a laser that shot out of the helium escape valve, and a remote detonator for bombs that, after activating, set off a blinking light at 12 o'clock on the dial. Bond used the laser to cut open the floor in the armoured express in order to free himself from the clutches of Alec Trevelyan (the renegade agent 006, who in the film wore a Seamaster himself – though an older model). The detonator came into its own somewhat later, when it was time to set off the bomb with which the Cuban command centre for the secret satellites activated by Goldeneye was to be destroyed.

**Rado**
Original diver, steel, automatic, ETA calibre 2824-2, water-resistant to 300 m (985 ft), unidirectional rotating inner divers' bezel, from 2006

**Rolex**
Oyster Perpetual Submariner, steel, automatic, Rolex calibre 1520, water-resistant to 200 m (657 ft), unidirectional rotating divers' bezel, service watch for Royal Marines frogmen, from 1969

**Rolex**
Oyster Perpetual Submariner, steel, automatic, Rolex calibre 1030, water-resistant to 200 m (657 ft), unidirectional rotating divers' bezel, from 1959

**Rolex**
Oyster Perpetual Submariner, steel, automatic, water-resistant to 200 m (657 ft), unidirectional rotating divers' bezel, from 1964

In the 1997 Bond film, *Tomorrow Never Dies*, the Seamaster acted as a detonator once again, setting off a grenade on the stealth boat belonging to media mogul Elliot Carver, the villain of the film, to make it visible on radar. In *The World is Not Enough*, the watch twice plays a decisive part. The first time, it is a strong light source, radiating from the dial of the Bond watch and used by Bond to gain a view of the situation inside his 'inflatable' jacket airbag in which he finds protection from the avalanche thundering over him. The second part was played by a grappling hook concealed in the case, allowing Bond to free himself and Dr Christmas Jones from the bunker. The miniature grappling hook shoots out from the crown and sets the rotating Seamaster bezel to race around furiously; as soon as the hook has caught firmly, the bezel turns slowly in the opposite direction, once more rolling up the wire within the watch case and drawing Bond and his companion upwards to safety.

## Important Dates in the History of Divers' Watches

**1927:** Rolex, with the Oyster, presents the first water-resistant watch case. As public proof of and advertising for this novelty, Rolex equips the swimmer Mercedes Gleitze with an Oyster, and she swims the English Channel with the watch on her wrist.

Left: Recognizable at first glance:
three of Rolex's divers' chronometers

**Scalfaro**
North Shore Chronograph TriCompax, steel, automatic, ADK calibre 150 (base ETA 7750), water-resistant to 100 m (328 ft), unidirectional rotating divers' bezel, from 2006

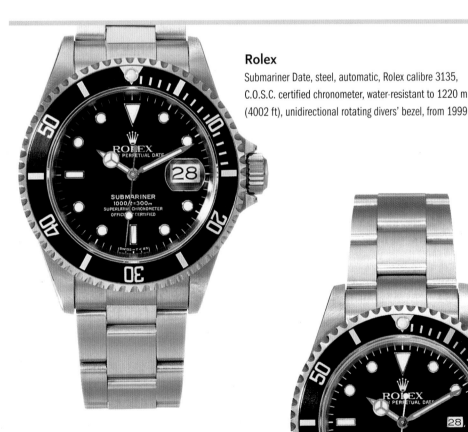

**Rolex**
Submariner Date, steel, automatic, Rolex calibre 3135, C.O.S.C. certified chronometer, water-resistant to 1220 m (4002 ft), unidirectional rotating divers' bezel, from 1999

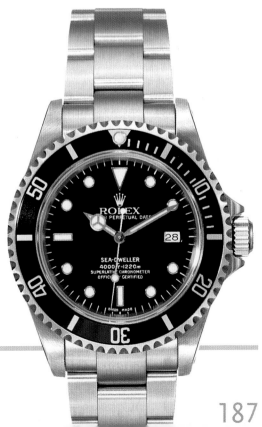

**Rolex**
Oyster Perpetual Sea Dweller 4000, steel, automatic, Rolex calibre 3135, C.O.S.C. certified chronometer, water-resistant to 1220 m (4002 ft), unidirectional rotating divers' bezel, helium valve in case, from 2006

**Scalfaro**
North Shore Second Time Zone, steel, automatic, ADK calibre 148 (base ETA 2892-2), 24-hour indicator (second zone time), water-resistant to 300 m (985 ft), unidirectional rotating divers' bezel, from 2006

187

**Sinn**
Divers' Chronograph, steel, automatic, ETA calibre 7750, water-resistant to 300 m (985 ft), case completely filled with argon gas, unidirectional rotating divers' bezel, screw-down push buttons, from 1999

**Sinn**
Einsatzzeitmesser (EZM 1), titanium, automatic, Lémania calibre 5100, water-resistant to 300 m (985 ft), chronograph, unidirectional rotating divers' bezel, from 1999

**1932:** Omega constructs its first water-resistant divers' watch, the Marine.

**1936:** Officine constructs the first prototype of a divers' watch, building a Rolex movement into the case of a Panerai depth meter.

**1953:** Blancpain launches the Fifty Fathoms, water-resistant to almost 100 metres (328 feet) (50 fathoms = 91.45 metres/300 feet). It was first made for the French navy. In 1959, frogmen of the German Bundeswehr were equipped with this watch. In the same year, the Zodiac Sea Wolf came out, exclusively issued for combat divers (US Seals). 1953 is also the birthday of what is probably the best-known divers' watch in the world: the Rolex Submariner.

**1954:** The Rolex Submariner is certified to 200 meters (657 feet) diving depth.

**1956:** The Blancpain Fifty Fathoms, due to its appearance in the Jacques Cousteau film, *The Silent World*, becomes known among sports divers. The Tudor Sub, with Rolex movement, appears in two versions, for 100 and 200 metres (328 and 657 feet) depth.

**1957:** The Omega Seamaster is launched (water-resistant to 200 metres/657 feet).

**1958:** The Breitling Superocean, also water-resistant to 200 metres (657 feet), appears on the market.

**1960:** As proof of its competence, Rolex manufactures a one-off timepiece with particularly thick glass, which, fastened to the outer shell of Jacques Piccard's submarine *Trieste*, survived a 10,916 metre (35,815 feet) dive unharmed.

**1961:** The Swiss diving expert, Hannes Keller, achieves a record diving depth of 220 metres (722 feet) with the divers' alarm Vulcain Cricket Nautical.

**Sinn**
Arktis divers' chronograph, steel, automatic, ETA calibre 7750, water-resistant to 300 m (985 ft), case completely filled with argon gas, lubrication with special oil for temperatures between –45 to 80 degrees C (–113 degrees Fahrenheit to 176 degrees Fahrenheit), unidirectional rotating divers' bezel, from 2006

**Stowa**
Seatime, steel, automatic, ETA calibre 2824, water-resistant to 300 m (985 ft), unidirectional rotating divers' bezel, from 2006

## TAG Heuer

Aquaracer Automatic Chronograph, steel, automatic, TAG Heuer calibre 16 (base ETA 7750), water-resistant to 300 m (985 ft), unidirectional rotating divers' bezel, from 2006

## Sinn

Einsatzzeitmesser (EZM 2), steel, quartz, ETA calibre 955.612, water-resistant to all reachable diving depths, case completely filled with oil, unidirectional rotating divers' bezel, from 2006

## Sinn

U1 divers' watch, submarine steel, automatic, ETA calibre 2824-2, water-resistant to 1000 m (3280 ft), unidirectional rotating divers' bezel, from 2006

## Sinn

U2/EZM5 divers' watch, submarine steel, automatic, ETA calibre 2893-2, 24-hour indicator (second zone time), water-resistant to 2000 m (6560 ft), unidirectional rotating divers' bezel, from 2006

## TAG Heuer

Aquagraph Automatic Chronograph, steel, automatic, TAG Heuer calibre 60 (based on Dubois-Dépraz 2073), water-resistant to 500 m (1640 ft), push buttons functional to 500 m (1640 ft) depth, stop-second and stop-minute from the centre, unidirectional rotating divers' bezel, from 2006

**Tissot**
Visodate Seamaster T12, steel,
automatic, calibre 784-2,
unidirectional rotating inner divers'
bezel, from 1975

**Tissot**
PR 100 Divermatic, steel, automatic,
ETA calibre 2836-2, water-resistant
to 150 m (492 ft), unidirectional
rotating divers' bezel, from 1999

**1963:** The Aquastar Benthos 500 is launched and accompanies the divers of the Précontinente-Experimente from Jacques-Yves Cousteau's team.

**1964:** The first divers' watches that can reach a depth of 1000 metres (3280 feet) are introduced. The one is the reworked Aquastar/Lemania Benthos and the other the Caribbean 1000.

**1965:** The Doxa brand is the first to target sports divers directly and introduces the Doxa Sub 300 at the Basle Clock and Watch Fair – the first divers' watch to have a clearly legible orange-coloured dial. Jaeger-LeCoultre presents the divers' alarm Polaris with an inner divers' bezel. Seiko introduces the first Japanese divers' watch (water-resistant to 150 metres/492 feet).

**1966:** With the Favre-Leuba Bathy 50, Henry Favre brings the first divers' watch with a Boyle-Marriot depth meter on to the market. In the USA, the watch is known as the Bathy 160 (because of its 160 feet diving depth).

**1967:** The bezel on the Doxa Sub 300, developed in cooperation with US divers, is patented. It gives information on decompression times. In the USA the Doxa is now used by the military. Rolex makes a Submariner with helium valve for professional use (Comex). Seiko improves the water resistance of its divers' watch and now calls it Professional 300. IWC launches its first divers' watch, the Aquatimer.

**1969:** Doxa's 200 T-Graph is the first divers' chronograph with a stopwatch mechanism which can be used underwater.

**1970:** For eight days, the new Omega Seamaster 600 accompanies three Comex divers saturation diving in 250 metres (820 feet) of water off Corsica. Diving pioneer Claude Wesley, in a dive in the Red Sea, tests prototypes by Doxa and Rolex with helium valves. In the same year, Doxa brings the production-ready Sub 600 Conquistador with helium valve on to the market.

**Tissot**
Seastar 1000 Automatic, steel, automatic, ETA calibre 2824-2, water-resistant to 300 m (985 ft), unidirectional rotating divers' bezel, from 2006

Right: A striking appearance: Divers' watch by Harry Winston. This jeweller and producer of decorative watches also understands decided masculine design

**TAG Heuer**
Kirium Chronometer, steel, automatic, ETA calibre 2892-A2, C.O.S.C. certified chronometer, water-resistant to 200 m (657 ft), unidirectional rotating divers' bezel, from 1999

## Tudor

Oyster Prince Submariner, steel, automatic, water-resistant to 200 m (657 ft), unidirectional rotating divers' bezel, from 1965

Left: To make a high-quality watch suitable for serious diving use, a great deal of time and money must be invested in the technology

## Tudor

Prince Date Hydronaut, steel, automatic, ETA calibre 2824-2, water-resistant to 200 m (657 ft), unidirectional rotating divers' bezel, from 2006

**1971:** Omega makes the Seamaster 1000. The Rolex Seadweller with helium valve (water-resistant to 610 metres/2001 feet) makes its appearance.

**1972:** Omega brings out its first chronograph that can also be used underwater (water-resistant to 120 metres/394 feet).

**1973:** The Doxa Sub 250 makes its appearance, the first with the crown at the four o'clock position.

**1975:** Seiko doubles the diving depth of its divers' watch to 600 metres (1970 feet) and is the first to use titanium in the construction of the case. The rubber strap, with its three expansion folds, is another innovation.

**1980:** IWC is commissioned by the German Bundeswehr to develop and make a divers' watch. The Nautilus brand introduces functional divers' watches at favourable prices: the Professional with a diving depth of 500 metres (1640 feet) for around 500 German marks and the Superpro with a diving depth of 1000 metres (3280 feet) for around 1000 marks.

**1983:** Sinn launches its first divers' watch, water-resistant to 1000 metres (3280 feet).

**1984:** The German Bundeswehr's research and development contract leads to the creation of the IWC Ocean 2000, the first divers' watch in the world that is water-resistant to 2000 metres (6560 feet). It is made in a military version (for the German navy) and a civilian version. A parallel amagnetic version is developed for mine divers, water resistant to 300 metres (985 feet).

**1985:** The Citizen Aquaband is the first analogue divers' watch with a digital electronic depth meter. Seiko also brings out a divers' watch with electronic depth meter, which is, however, considerably larger than the Citizen.

**1986:** TAG Heuer launches the Super Professional model for dive depths of 1000 metres (3280 feet).

## Tutima

DI 300, titanium, automatic, ETA calibre 2836-2, water-resistant to 300 m (985 ft), unidirectional rotating divers' bezel, from 2006

## Ulysse Nardin

Maxi Marine Diver Chronometer, steel, automatic, Ulysse Nardin calibre UN26 (base ETA 2892), C.O.S.C. certified chronometer, water-resistant to 300 m (985 ft), from 2006

**Universal Genève**
Golden Tech Diver, steel/gold, automatic, Universal Genève calibre 71, unidirectional rotating divers' bezel, water-resistant to 100 m (328 ft), from 1999

**Louis Vuitton**
Tambour Diving Automatique XL, rose gold, automatic, ETA calibre 2895-2, water-resistant to 300 m (985 ft), unidirectional rotating divers' bezel, from 2006

**1987:** Casio also introduces a watch with electronic depth meter, but with fully digital display only, in contrast to Citizen.

**1988:** The Citizen Aqualand continues to be improved and now has a second display and more compact sensor.

**1989:** The Rolex Submariner now has a divers' bezel that rotates anticlockwise only. The Citizen Aqualand is now also available with analogue depth meter display. The Citizen Aqualand becomes the favourite watch among sports divers.

**1993:** Omega designs a dive chronometer for depths of up to 300 metres (9850 feet). The free-diver Roland Specker, wearing this watch, achieves a world record depth of 80 metres (262 feet) in Lake Neufchatel. In the same year, Omega launches the Seamaster Professional, a watch still up-to-date today, with its helium valve. An appearance in a James Bond film causes the Seamaster to become known as the Bond watch.

**1995:** Breitling makes the Colt Superocean for a dive depth of up to 1500 metres (4920 feet).

**1996:** Kienzle breaks the Rolex world depth record with The Deepest. This record-breaker is a simple plastic timepiece filled with oil to stabilize it. Its depth capacity is certified to 12,000 metres (39,370 feet). Sector introduces the Diving Team 1000 for depths of up to 1000 metres (3280 feet).

**1997:** The Finnish manufacturer Suunto presents the Spyder, the first diving computer in watch format, which becomes very popular among divers.

**1998:** IWC introduces the GST Aquatimer for depths of up to 2000 metres (6560 feet).

**1999:** IWC launches the Deep One, the first divers' watch with mechanical depth gauge and split-second hand. It indicates depths of up to 45 metres (148 feet) and is water-resistant to 150 metres (492 feet).

**Vulcain**
Cricket Nautical, steel, hand winding, calibre MSR S 2, water-resistant to 300 m (985 ft), dial centre with bidirectional rotation for dive decompression times, alarm, from 1969

**2000:** Ulysse Nardin presents the first mechanical divers' watch with perpetual calendar.

**2002:** Breitling launches the Avenger Seawolf for depths of up to 3000 metres (9850 feet) and holds the current world record for mechanical watches.

**2003:** TAG Heuer launches the 2000 Aquagraph model, the first divers' chronograph that remains functional at depths of up to 500 metres (1640 feet). Baume & Mercier (CapeLand S XXl 1000) and Oris (TT1 Master Diver) bring out watches for depths of up to 1000 metres (3280 feet), the new Bvlgari models (Diagono Professional Scuba Diving 2000) and Mühle (SAR Rescue Timer) are tested to 200 metres (657 feet). Doxa begins production of the Sub 600 again, after the limited edition of the Sub 300 was sold out in a very short time.

**2004:** IWC introduces the Aquatimer Split Minute Chronograph, the first watch with a split-second hand that can be used under water.

**2006:** Eterna launches the KonTiki Diver, a divers' watch with a unique case structure. The watch can only be adjusted with the case open.

## Harry Winston
Ocean, platinum, automatic, GP calibre 3106, divers' bezel (unidirectional rotation), water-resistant to 100 m (328 ft), from 1999

## Vulcain
Nautical, steel, hand winding, Vulcain calibre V-10, water-resistant to 300 m (985 ft), dial centre with bidirectional rotation for dive decompression times, alarm, from 2006

## Zenith
Rainbow Elite divers' watch, steel, automatic, Zenith calibre Elite, unidirectional rotating divers' bezel, water-resistant to 200 m (657 ft), from 1999

# 5. GMT AND WORLD TIME WATCHES

In other countries, they do things differently. They often have a different time, for instance. If you are in business, or are a jetsetter or globetrotter, it's a good idea to wear a watch that tells you what the time is at your destination, but won't let you forget the time at home.

## Alpina

Avalanche GMT, steel, quartz,
24-hour indicator (second zone time),
from 2006

## Baume and Mercier

Classima Executives GMT XL, steel,
automatic, BM calibre 11893-2
(base ETA 2893-2) 24-hour indicator
(second zone time), from 2006

The world is a sphere, more or less. Because this sphere turns around the sun, only half of it is ever lit at any one time. Today this seems obvious, but until the mid-nineteenth century little attention was paid to this fact, according to which time would have to be different in different places across the world.

In Germany alone, each of the many princedoms had its own time. This could perhaps be tolerated in the age of stagecoaches, but after the introduction of the transregional, and above all much faster, railways led to utter chaos. Just imagine a rail timetable that had to take account of more than 30 different local times!

In a small country such as Germany, this caused difficulties enough, but in countries that extended farther to the east and west, such as Russia, for example, or the USA, it led to even greater problems. After lengthy international negotiations, there was agreement in 1884 on

## Audemars Piguet

Millenary Dual Time, yellow gold, automatic, AP calibre 2129, additional 12-hour indicator (second zone time), power reserve indicator, from 1999

## Blancpain

GMT, steel, automatic, Blancpain calibre 5A50, 24-hour indicator (second zone time), rotating bezel with 24-hour time division (third zone time), from 1999

the division of the earth into 24 time zones. This regulation, however, was not accepted until the beginning of the last century. Established in the UK to regularize national railway timetables, and later adopted internationally, this regulation was known as GMT (Greenwich Mean Time) since the Greenwich Meridian (0° longitude) is the starting point for the time zones. It is now known as UTC, Coordinated Universal Time, the main feature of which is the use of the 24-hour clock as applied to the time zones.

GMT and UTC are in general use today in the clockmaking industry as a term for timepieces covering two or more time zones. The Rolex GMT Master II, for example, has a 24-hour hand constantly set to home time, but also, if selected, GMT. Local time is shown by the hour hand, which can be set without moving the minute hand. The second hand also continues to run, thus not losing a single second for the watch-lover. The IWC Spitfire UTC functions in a similar manner, the only difference being that the 24-hour display is here shown in a semicircular cut-out of the dial.

One small snag with GMT watches is that the owner needs to know the time difference

**Blancpain**
Le Brassus GMT Moon Phase, red gold, automatic, Blancpain calibre 67A6, 24-hour indicator (second zone time), from 2006

**Rainer Brand**
Panama Dual Time, steel, automatic, ETA calibre 2892-2, additional 12-hour indicator (second zone time), from 1999

**Rainer Brand**
Panama Dual Time, steel, automatic, ETA calibre 2892-2, additional 12-hour indicator (second zone time), from 2006

**Blancpain**
Léman Réveil GMT, red gold, automatic, Blancpain calibre 1241, 24-hour indicator (second zone time), alarm function, from 2006

**Breguet**
Marine GMT, yellow gold, automatic, Breguet calibre 563, world time indicator, from 1999

199

**Carl F. Bucherer**

Patravi Travel Tec GMT, steel, automatic, CFB calibre 1901, 24-hour indicator and rotating bezel under glass with 24-hour divisions (second and third zone times), chronograph, from 2006

**Carl F. Bucherer**

Patravi Chronograph GMT, steel, automatic, CFB calibre 1901, 24-hour indicator and rotating bezel with 24-hour divisions (second and third zone times), chronograph, from 2006

**Breitling**

B-1, steel, quartz, Breitling calibre 78, 24-hour Indicator (second zone time), chronograph, alarm function, C.O.S.C. certified chronometer, from 2006

**Breitling**

Colt GMT, steel, automatic, Breitling calibre 32 (base ETA 2893-2), 24-hour indicator (second zone time), C.O.S.C. certified chronometer, from 2006

between home and local time. Going right around the whole world (in timekeeping terms) requires a world time watch. Its decisive external feature is an adjustable ring with the name of one place within each of the 24 time zones of our world, and in most cases also a 24-hour indicator. It sounds simple, but technically it is not without snags, which arise as soon as we come to the setting of date and time. When crossing the date line in the Pacific, for example, the date display also needs to be put back, along with the city and 24-hour bezel.

**Bulova**
Edition, steel, automatic, ETA calibre 2892, 24-hour indicator (second zone time), power reserve indicator, from 1999

**Bvlgari**
Diagono Professional GMT Fly-Back, steel, automatic, Dubois-Dépraz calibre 21340, 24-hour indicator (second zone time), chronograph with Fly-Back function, C.O.S.C. certified chronometer, from 2006

**Bvlgari**
Bvlgari GMT, steel, automatic, calibre MVA 060, 24-hour indicator (second zone time), from 1999

### Chopard

L.U.C. GMT, white gold, automatic,
L.U.C. calibre 4/96/1-H1, 24-hour
indicator (second zone time),
C.O.S.C. certified chronometer,
from 2006

### Corum

Classical GMT, steel, automatic, Corum
calibre CO 983983, (base ETA 2892-A2 with
module), 24-hour indicator (second zone
time), rotating bezel with names of reference
cities for time zones, C.O.S.C. certified
chronometer, from 2006

### Chronoswiss

Tora, yellow gold, automatic,
Chronoswiss calibre C.123, 24-hour
indicator (second zone time),
from 1999

### Cuervo y Sobrinos

Prominente D.T., steel, automatic, ETA
calibre 2671, additional 12-hour indicator
(second zone time), from 2006

Clever engineers and watch designers have come up with all kinds of mechanisms and levers, to solve this problem, which can be used with push buttons on the case, a second crown, or a rotating bezel.

## Individual world time

In 2004 Vogard brought a watch on to the market that has exclusively (so far) devoted itself to the topic of 'world time'. The mechanism, devised by Vogard and now patented, allows the simple operation of a bezel, well-known from divers' watches and chronographs, to set the desired time zone. The design is based on seeing the case, movement and bezel as a single functioning unit.

A noticeable exterior feature of the design by Thomas Prescher, and at the same time a decisive functioning part, is the crescent-shaped lever which moves on a screwed-in hinge by the lower right strap holder. In the rest position, the lever lies in an enclosure within the case.

**Davosa**
Vireo Dual Time, steel, automatic, ETA calibre 2893, 24-hour indicator (second zone time), from 2006

**Jaquet Droz**
Les Deux Fuseaux, white gold, automatic, Jaquet Droz calibre 5L60, 24-hour indicator (second zone time), from 2006

**De Grisogono**
Instrumento Doppio Tre, steel, automatic, ETA calibre 2892-A2 with module and hand movement at rear, additional 12-hour indicator on back of case, from 2006

**De Witt**
Académia Double Fuseau, red gold, automatic, De Witt calibre DW 2001 (base ETA 2892-A2), 24-hour indicator (second zone time), from 2006

**Dubey & Schaldenbrand**
Diplomatic Classic, steel, automatic,
ETA calibre 2892-A2, 24-hour
indicator (second zone time),
from 1999

If the lever is moved out from the case, a button springs out, activated by a powerful spring, to protrude by about 1.8 mm (0.1 inches) from the case. This then releases the bezel, previously held by a projection on the flank of the button.

The bezel (city ring) is available from Vogard marked with various destinations, such as major cities, airports, or even golf courses. You can even have one-off versions with a customized selection of places. You can have a bezel made with the names of places you have visited, of cities in which your friends live, or just have Berlin replace Paris for 'Central European Time'.

**Dubey & Schaldenbrand**
Aerodyn Duo, steel, automatic, ETA calibre 2893, 24-hour
indicator (second zone time), from 2006

**Dubey & Schaldenbrand**
Diplomatic GMT, steel, automatic,
ETA calibre 2892-A2, 24-hour
indicator (second zone time),
from 1999

**Roger Dubuis**
Golden Square Dual Time, rose gold,
automatic, RD calibre 5747, additional
12-hour indicator (second zone time),
from 2006

## Enicar
Sherpa Jet Automatic, steel, automatic, calibre AR 116, 24-hour indicator with rotating bezel under glass (second zone time), from 1975

## Ebel
Sportwave Meridian, steel, automatic, Ebel calibre 122 (base ETA 2892-A2), 24-hour indicator (second zone time), from 1999

## Ebel
Sportwave GMT, steel, automatic, Ebel calibre 123 (base ETA 2893-2), 24-hour indicator (second zone time), from 2006

## Ebel
Voyager, steel, automatic, Ebel calibre 124 (base ETA 2892-A2), world time indicator, from 1999

## Louis Erard
Power reserve/second time zone, steel, automatic, calibre ER 61, 24-hour indicator (second zone time), from 1999

## Pilot's watches – with a difference

There can hardly be a professional group for whom it makes more sense to have a world time watch than pilots and other 'frequent fliers' who incessantly cross the globe – which is why there is such a watch in the 'Lufthansa Collection' of the Saxony-based German company Nautische Instrumente Mühle Glashütte. The most noticeable feature of this watch is an additional crown integrated into the lower strap holder of the stainless steel case. It serves to set the inner rotating bezel with the printed names of a place in each time zone. In this watch, the task of the rotating bezel with 24-hour divisions has been taken over by an orange lacquered pointer. Moving at half the speed of the hour hand, it brushes a delicate ring of figures printed on the black dial between the bezel with the names of cities and the minutes ring.

**Eterna**
KonTiki GMT, steel, automatic, ETA calibre 2893-2, 24-hour indicator (second zone time), from 2006

**Fortis**
Official Cosmonauts' Sport Pilot GMT, steel, automatic, ETA calibre 2893-2, 24-hour indicator (second zone time), from 1999

**Formex**
Diver GMT, steel/titanium, automatic, ETA calibre 2892-A2, 24-hour indicator (second zone time), water-resistant to 300 m (985 feet), from 2006

**Fortis**
Pilot Professional GMT, steel, automatic, ETA calibre 2893-2, 24-hour indicator (second zone time), from 1999

## Fortis

B-42 Official Cosmonauts' GMT, steel, automatic, ETA calibre 2893-2, 24-hour indicator (second zone time), from 2006

## Fortis

B-42 Chrono GMT, ETA calibre 7750, 24-hour indicator (second zone time), chronograph, C.O.S.C. certified chronometer, from 2006

## Fortis

Flieger GMT, steel, automatic, ETA calibre 2893-2, 24-hour indicator (second zone time), from 2006

Below: Overview of world time zones

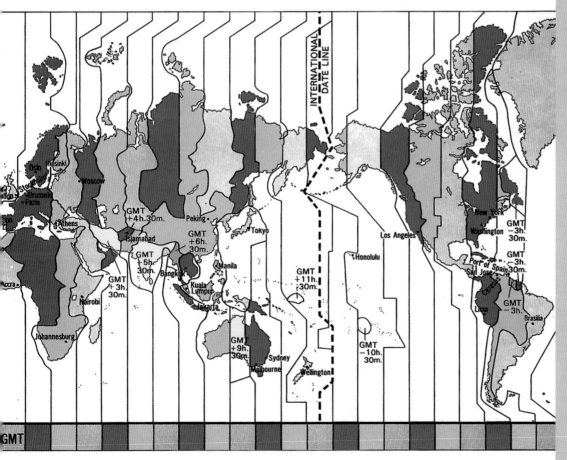

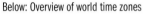

## Gérald Genta

Night & Day, yellow gold, automatic, GG calibre 1961 (base ETA 2892-A2), second hour hand plus day/night indicator (second zone time), from 1999

207

**Glycine**

Airman 7, steel, automatic, three independent ETA calibres, one with additional 24-hour indicator (four zone times), from 2006

**Girard-Perregaux**

GMT, white gold, GP calibre, separately adjustable second hour hand (second zone time)

**Glycine**

Airman 9, steel, automatic, ETA calibre 7754, 24-hour indicator (second zone time), chronograph, from 2006

**Girard-Perregaux**

ww.tc Chronograph, white gold, automatic, GP calibre 3387, 24-hour indicator with bezel under glass (second zone time), chronograph, from 2006

**Girard-Perregaux**

Vintage King Size Chrono GMT, rose gold, automatic, GP calibre 033C0, 24-hour indicator (second zone time), chronograph, from 2006

## From Boston to Hamburg? Press six times!

In 2000, Patek Philippe returned to the long tradition of the brand as a producer of world time watches, though this was a tradition they had not maintained for decades. Not least for that reason, Patek Philippe watches of this type today sell at auction for astronomical prices.

The new world time watch shows local time in all the world's 24 time zones at a glance and is distinguished by being particularly user-friendly: two concentric rings turn about the central dial where minute and hour hands show local time. The inner has a 24-hour display with

**Heuer**
Autavia GMT, steel, automatic, calibre 12, 24-hour indicator (second zone time), from 1975

**Michel Herbelin**
Newport J-Class GMT, steel, automatic, ETA calibre 2892 with module, 24-hour indicator (second zone time), power reserve indicator, from 2006

**IWC**
Aviator watch UTC, steel, automatic, IWC calibre C.37526, digital 24-hour indicator (second zone time), from 1999

**Ikepod**
Seaslug, steel, automatic, ETA calibre 2893-2, 24-hour indicator (second zone time), from 1999

209

**Jaeger-LeCoultre**
Reverso Géographique, steel,
automatic, JLC calibre 858, rotatable
city ring under glass on back of case
(world time), day/night indicator,
from 1999

**Jaeger-LeCoultre**
Reverso Grande GMT, steel, automatic, JLC calibre 878,
second time indicator plus day/night display on back
of case (second zone time), chronograph, from 2006

**Jaeger-LeCoultre**
Reverso Duoface, steel, automatic, JLC calibre 929/3,
second 12-hour indicator on back of case (second zone time),
from 1999

**Jaeger-LeCoultre**
Reverso Grande Automatique, steel,
automatic, JLC calibre 970,
adjustable second hour hand plus
day/night indicator (second zone
time), from 2006

**Jaeger-LeCoultre**
Master Geographic, red gold, automatic, JLC calibre 929/3,
rotatable city ring under glass on back of case (world time),
from 1999

**Jaeger-LeCoultre**
Master Geographic, steel, automatic, JLC calibre 929/3,
rotatable city ring under glass on back of case (world time),
from 1999

day and night phases marked, while the outer is inscribed with 24 place names symbolizing the different time zones. These two rings can be used at any time to read the current time in the 24 time zones. The numbers 1 to 24 are in each case positioned under a place name in the time zone concerned. The place and time with day/night display that can be seen above the pointer (shaped like an arrow) at the '12' correspond to the local time indicated by minute and hour hands.

Setting the watch is very easy. The user, for example, is in Paris at eight in the morning and wants to reset the watch. To do this, he or she

**Jaeger-LeCoultre**
Master Compressor Geographic, steel, automatic, JLC calibre 923, rotating city ring under glass plus AM/PM indicator (world time), from 2006

**Jaeger-LeCoultre**
Master Hometime, steel, automatic, JLC calibre 975, adjustable second hour hand plus day/night indicator (second zone time), from 2006

**Jaeger-LeCoultre**
Master Extreme World Chronograph, titanium, automatic, JLC calibre 923, rotating under glass city bezel plus AM/PM indicator (world time), chronograph, patented shock absorber system, from 2006

**Jaeger-LeCoultre**
Master Compressor Dualmatic, steel, automatic, JLC calibre 972, adjustable second hour hand plus 24-hour indicator (second zone time), from 2006

**Kelek**
Chronograph with second time zone, steel, automatic, Kelek calibre 7752, second separately adjustable hour hand (second zone time), from 1999

**F.P. Journe**
Chronomètre à Resonnance, platinum, hand winding, F.P. Journe calibre 1499-2, second 12-hour indicator, from 2006

**Kurth**
Jubilee World Time Chrono No. 2, steel, automatic, ETA calibre 7750, rotating city ring under glass, chronograph, from 2006

presses the button on the left edge of the case at ten o'clock often enough to move Paris on to the 12 o'clock position. Then, as with every other watch, he or she sets the hands to eight o'clock using the winding crown. The whole 24-hour ring will now turn. The watch owner has to take care that the figure 8 (and not the 20) comes to be under the place name 'Paris'. Once this adjustment has been made, the crown is no longer used for adjustments.

## Two days, two nights

It's not always necessary to make new discoveries from scratch to create something special. This has been proved again and again in recent years by the A. Lange & Söhne factory, which has demonstrated,

with impressive inventions, how everyday timepiece features, such as a date display, can be turned into technical treasures.

A world time watch is, of course, more complicated. After all, it is expected to display several zone times, preferably one for each of the 24 time zones. The Lange 1 Time Zone meets this demand in the classic manner, having a 'city ring', the typical feature of a world time watch, around the edge of the main dial.

Two pairs of hands can be adjusted independently on the corresponding dials. According to the design principle on which Lange 1 is based, these are asymmetrically arranged. The display of the second zone time is on a subsidiary dial, with Arabic numbers,

## Maurice Lacroix

Masterpiece Double Rétrograde, rose gold, hand winding, ML calibre 100 (base ETA 6498), digital second hour indicator (second zone time), from 1999

## Maurice Lacroix

2ième Temps, steel/yellow gold, automatic, ML calibre 29 (base ETA 2836-2), 24-hour indicator (second zone time), retrograde date indicator, from 2006

## Longines

Master Collection GMT, steel, automatic, Longines calibre L635 (base ETA 2824-2), 24-hour indicator (second zone time), from 2006

## Minerva

Palladio Dual Time, steel, automatic, Minerva calibre 24 DT, 24-hour indicator, chronograph, from 1999

## A. Lange & Söhne

Lange 1 Time Zone, red gold, hand winding, Lange calibre L031.1, rotating city bezel plus day/night indicator (world time), from 2006

## Movado

Polygraph, steel, hand winding, 24-hour indicator (second zone time), from 1960

## Montblanc

Masterpiece Dual Time, steel/gold, ETA calibre 2892-A2, 24-hour indicator (second zone time), from 1999

## Montblanc

Time Walker GMT, steel, automatic, Montblanc calibre 4810/405 (base ETA 2893-2), 24-hour indicator (second zone time), from 2006

## Franck Müller

Cintrée Curvex World Time, yellow gold, automatic, FM calibre 2800, 24-hour indicator (second zone time), from 1999

## Mühle Glashütte

Traveller Automatic, steel, automatic, ETA calibre 2892-A2, 24-hour indicator (second zone time), from 1999

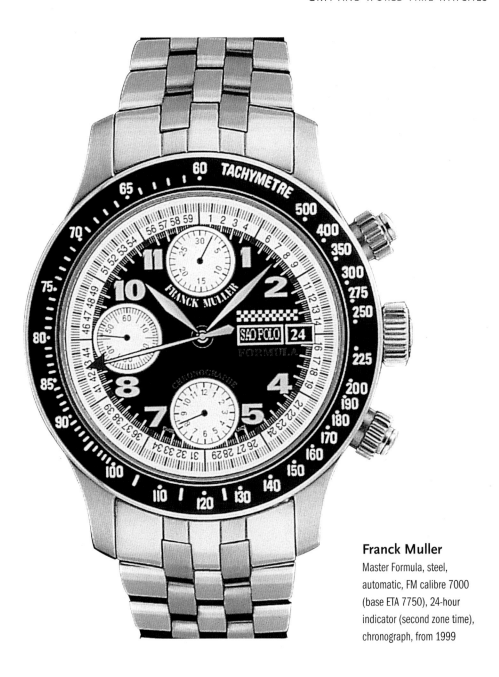

**Franck Muller**
Master Formula, steel, automatic, FM calibre 7000 (base ETA 7750), 24-hour indicator (second zone time), chronograph, from 1999

**Franck Muller**
Master Banker, steel, automatic, FM calibre 2800, second 12-hour indicator (second zone time), from 1999

**Omega**
Seamaster GMT, steel, automatic, Omega calibre 1128 (base ETA 2892-A2), 24-hour indicator (second zone time), C.O.S.C. certified chronometer, from 1999

which has taken the position of the little seconds indicator dial in the Lange 1. The large subsidiary dial, with its gold Roman hour markings, provides the home time.

Each ring of figures has a day/night indicator, essential for time zone watches, added to it. Their tiny pointers run synchronously.

Two buttons for adjustment on the left of the case serve to set the large date and the individual world timepiece functions. Normally, when setting out on a journey, the city ring is set with the aid of the button at '8'. This makes the ring inscribed with the names of 24 representative places in the individual time zones move round – viewed geographically – one time zone further to the east with each push. The hour hand of the subsidiary dial with the Arabic numbers also moves around correspondingly in this process, as does the day/night indicator.

**Oris**
Worldtimer, steel, automatic, Oris calibre 690 (base ETA 2836-2), second 12-hour indicator (second zone time), moon phase indicator, from 1999

**Oris**
Atelier Complication, steel, automatic, Oris calibre 4810/581 (base ETA 2688/2671), 24-hour indicator (second zone time), moon phase indicator, from 2006

**Oris**
Big Crown Complication, steel, automatic, Oris calibre 581 (base ETA 2688/2671), 24-hour indicator (second zone time), from 2006

**Parmigiani**
Toric Répétition Minutes GMT, rose gold, hand winding, Parmigiani calibre 251, 24-hour indicator (second zone time), quarter hour and minute repetition, from 2006

# Of time zones and zone times

Our world is officially divided into 24 time zones, counting eastwards from the zero meridian. This is due to the east-west rotation of the Earth, which turns anticlockwise as seen from the north pole and clockwise as seen from the south pole. A world time watch can be set to each of the time zones. It cannot display the time zone itself, which is, after all, geographically defined and not a time term. It therefore displays the time of the zone of the Earth for which the watch has been set. The customary term of a watch with a 'second time zone', often used in connection with GMT watches, is understandable therefore, but incorrect. To be correct, the reference when listing what a GMT or world time watch can show would have to be to a 'second' or 'third' 'zone time'.

## Patek Philippe

World time watch, rose gold, automatic, Patek Philippe calibre 240 HU, two counter-rotating dials with world cities and 24-hour display (world time), from 2006

## Patek Philippe

Calatrava Travel Time, yellow gold, hand winding, Patek Philippe calibre 215 PS FUS 24H, second, separately adjustable hour hand plus 24-hour indicator (second zone time), from 1999

## Paul Picot

Gentleman Chrono GMT, steel, automatic, PP calibre 8104 (base ETA 7750), 24-hour indicator (second zone time), from 2006

## Patek Philippe

Travel Time, yellow gold, hand winding, Patek Philippe calibre 215/156, second separately adjustable hour hand plus 24-hour indicator (second zone time), from 2006

## From the donkey to UTC

From ancient times onwards there have been maps showing the Earth with its surface divided into a network of longitude and latitude. Ptolemy, when creating his maps, placed the zero meridian in the region of the Canary Isles (today some 15 degrees longitude west). Later cartographers moved the zero meridian to Rome, Copenhagen, Paris, or St Petersburg, before it was finally 'moved' to London. As the Earth turns on its own axis, and every meridian makes a line between the north and south poles, the position of the zero meridian is in fact of no importance and was purely a political matter.

**Auguste Reymond**
Cotton Club Global Time, steel, automatic, ETA calibre 2893-2, 24-hour indicator (second zone time), from 1999

**Rolex**
GMT Master, steel, automatic, Rolex calibre 1030, 24-hour hand (second zone time), adjustable bezel with 24 divisions, C.O.S.C. certified chronometer, from 1956

**Rolex**
GMT Master, steel, automatic, Rolex calibre 3175 (base Rolex 3135), 24-hour hand (second zone time), adjustable bezel with 24 divisions, C.O.S.C. certified chronometer, from 1999

**Rolex**
Explorer, steel, automatic, Rolex calibre 3185 (base Rolex 3135), 24-hour hand (second zone time), C.O.S.C. certified chronometer, from 1999

### Rolex

GMT Master II, yellow gold, automatic, Rolex calibre 3185 (base Rolex 3135), 24-hour hand (second zone time), adjustable bezel with 24 divisions, C.O.S.C. certified chronometer, from 2006

### Schwarz Etienne

Chronograph GMT, steel, automatic, LIP calibre 8104 (base ETA 7750), 24-hour indicator (second zone time) chronograph, from 2006

### Schwarz Etienne

Carée, automatic, LIP calibre 8154 (base ETA 7750), 24-hour indicator (second zone time), chronograph, from 2006

### Daniel Roth

GMT, steel, automatic, modified GP calibre 3100, second digital hour indicator (second zone time), from 1999

**Sinn**

Multifunction Chronograph, steel, automatic, modified ETA calibre 7750, 24-hour indicator (second zone time), chronograph, from 2006

**Sinn**

Frankfurt World Time, steel, automatic, modified ETA calibre 2893-2, 24-hour indicator (second zone time), rotating bezel with 12 divisions under glass (third zone time), from 2006

**Sinn**

Aviator with magnetic field protection and second time zone, surface hardened steel, automatic, ETA calibre 2893-2, 24-hour display (second zone time), from 2006

**Sinn**

World Time Chronograph, steel, automatic, modified ETA calibre 7750, 24-hour indicator (second zone time), chronograph, from 1999

Seen against the background of how easily the expressions 'time zone' and 'zone time' can lead to misunderstandings, it is not hard to imagine the difficulties connected to the introduction of these terms.

The problems began with the dispute between the eternal rivals Great Britain and France about determining the zero meridian, which the one party naturally wanted in London and the other, of course, in Paris. After the Royal Observatory in the London suburb of Greenwich had already published a Nautical Almanac as early as 1767, the

**TAG Heuer**
Carrera Twin-Time, steel, automatic,
TAG Heuer calibre 7 (base ETA
2893-2), 24-hour indicator (second
time zone), from 2006

**Sothis**
World Time Chrono, steel, automatic,
modified ETA calibre 7750, reference
cities for time zones on the bezel under
glass, from 1999

**Temption**
Automat with second time zone, steel, automatic, ETA calibre
2893-2, 24-hour indicator (second zone time), from 1999

**Tiffany**
Streamamerica World Time, steel, automatic, ETA calibre, 2824-2,
world time indicator, from 1999

**Tiffany**
Classic Two Time Tonneau, steel,
quartz-controlled, ETA calibre
280.002, second 12-hour indicator,
from 1999

**Tutima**

Aviator Chronograph F2 UTC, steel, automatic, modified ETA calibre 7750, 24-hour indicator (second zone time), chronograph, from 2006

**Tissot**

Navigator Seastar T12, steel, automatic, calibre 798, 24-hour dial, rotating bezel under glass with names of reference cities for time zones (world time indicator), from 1975

**Tutima**

Automatic FX UTC, steel, automatic, ETA calibre 2893-2, 24-hour indicator (second zone time), from 2006

confident Anglo-Saxons decided that the zero meridian, the determining line for worldwide timekeeping, should run through the English capital. From then on, people spoke of 'Greenwich Mean Time' (GMT).

Countries spread out over a long distance east to west, such as Russia or the USA where there had been over 300 local times, naturally had the most problems with the many different local times. That might well be the reason why it was the American Meteorological Society that, in 1875, provided the impulse for creating a uniform time system valid worldwide, which was decided upon in 1884. The division of the Earth into 24 time zones followed. There was a difference of one hour from one time zone to the next, increasing as you moved from west to east and based on the zero meridian. Gradually, all countries joined this system. Even France eventually accepted London as the site of zero longitude.

As the day has 24 hours in which the world turns once, that is to say, describes a full circle of 360 degrees, a time zone covers 15 degrees of longitude (360 degrees divided by 24 = 15 degrees) – in theory.

In practice, there are considerably more time zones, for geographic and political reasons, because some countries want to have half-hourly divisions between time zones or have only one time zone, such as China, although they are gigantic countries. In addition, many countries do not have summer time, which would, in any case, make little sense in countries near to the equator, which have almost equal phases of light and dark.

Central European Time (CET) was introduced in 1893 and corresponds to Greenwich time plus one hour. The time zone stretches from the western shores of Spain to the eastern borders of Poland, covering a stretch of nearly 35 degrees longitude.

**Ulysse Nardin**
San Marco GMT +/–, steel, automatic, UN calibre 20, 24-hour indicator (second zone time), perpetual calendar, from 1999

**Ulysse Nardin**
Perpetual Calendar GMT +/–, white gold, automatic, UN calibre 32, 24-hour hand (second zone time), perpetual calendar, from 2006

**Ulysse Nardin**
GMT +/–, Big Date Dual Time, red gold, automatic, UN calibre 22, digital 24-hour indicator (second zone time), perpetual calendar, from 2006

**Universal Genève**
Janus, platinum/red gold, hand winding, Universal Genève calibre 42, double hour display plus day/night indicator (second zone time), reversible case, from 1999

**Victorinox**
AirBoss Mach 5, steel, automatic, ETA calibre 2893-2, 24-hour indicator (second zone time), from 2006

**Vacheron Constantin**
Royal Eagle Dual Time, white gold, automatic, Vacheron Constantin calibre 1222 H393, second 12-hour indicator plus day/night indicator (second zone time), from 2006

**Vacheron Constantin**
Malte Dual Time, rose gold, Vacheron Constantin calibre 1206 RDT, 24-hour indicator (second zone time), C.O.S.C. certified chronometer, from 2006

**Vulcain**
Aviator GMT, steel, hand winding, Vulcain calibre V-10, 24-hour indicator (second zone time), alarm function, from 2006

Since 1972 the International Telecommunication Union has used the abbreviation UTC, a compromise between CUT (Coordinated Universal Time) used by English speakers and TUC (Temps Universel Coordonné) used by French speakers. UTC has uniform seconds defined by International Atomic Time, with leap seconds introduced irregularly to compensate for discrepancies. UTC, used for atomic clocks, broadcast by short wave radios and via satellite, is also oriented to the zero meridian, but instead of using Anglo-Saxon descriptions such as '5 a.m'. for the morning and '5 p.m'. for the afternoon, time is given unambiguously in 24 hours. The four-digit form is used both in writing and when giving the spoken time. For example, one o'clock in the morning is UTC 0100; when spoken, it is 'zero one hundred'.

**Raymond Weil**
Don Giovanni Cosi Grande Two Time
Zones, steel, automatic, RW calibre
2200 (base ETA 2671), 24-hour
indicator (second zone time),
from 2006

**George J. von Burg**
GMT Fly-Back, steel automatic, GJVB
calibre 8107 (base ETA 7750), 24-hour
indicator (second zone time), chronograph
with Fly-Back function, from 2006

**Zenith**
Grande Class Power Reserve Dual Time, rose gold, automatic,
Zenith calibre 683 Elite, 24-hour indicator (second zone time),
power reserve display, from 2006

**Zenith**
Class Dual Time, steel, automatic, Zenith calibre 682 Elite,
24-hour indicator (second zone time), from 2006

**Harry Winston**
Greenwich, yellow gold, automatic,
second hour hand plus day/night
indicator (second zone time),
from 1999

# 6. WATCHES WITH ALARM FEATURES

Watches with alarm features were always exotic items, although today, when cheap digital watches and mobile phones have alarm functions, they are really only of interest to watch-lovers with a liking for extravagance.

**Certina**
Alarm, steel, automatic, calibre AS 5007, from 1976

**Cyma**
Time-o-Vox, steel/gold-plated, hand winding, Cyma calibre 464, from 1953

**Breguet**
Alarm watch, Le Réveil du Tsar, yellow gold, automatic, Breguet calibre 519 F, automatic winding of the alarm movement, 24-hour indicator (second zone time), from 2006

**Cartier**
Alarm watch, steel, hand winding, JLC calibre 489/1, from 1952

The few watches still on offer today with this delightful additional function usually have a type of movement devised back in the 1940s and 50s. New designs of alarm watches are rare. In the way they work, these small alarms have a good deal in common with their fat tin relatives, the ones that in years gone by stood on so many bedside tables and ticked so loudly it was difficult to get the sleep from which they were intended to wake one the following morning. It is of course one advantage of the alarm on your wrist that you can only hear it when it is intended to wake you.

Let's look at the function first. Under the hour wheel (to which the hour hand is attached) there is a leaf spring fastened to one end of the bottom plate. It covers the whole of this and protrudes into the movement on the other side. There are two cams on the hour wheel. The leaf spring forms a ring enclosing the set-hands arbour and from below gently presses the hour wheel in the direction of the dial. There is the alarm-set wheel, which can only be adjusted

from outside via the crown, and which has two small notches into which the hour wheel with its cams can fit if the hour wheel and the alarm-set wheel are in a particular relationship to one another. This point in time is the alarm time.

When the cams of the hour wheel slot into the notches in the alarm-set wheel, this moves the free end of the leaf spring slightly and thus releases the alarm hammer, previously blocked by the leaf spring. The hammer then strikes quickly against the back of the case or some other resonant body, making a rattling noise or a delicate ringing, and vibrating the watch on the wrist.

## A watch that lets its voice be heard

When watch-lovers talk about alarm wrist-watches, they often mention Memovox. This is the name of the alarm by Jaeger-LeCoultre, which has been part of their range – constantly being altered – since 1951. The name says it all, deriving as it does from the Latin words

## Eterna

1948 alarm, steel, automatic, base AS 5008, replica of the first Eterna-Matic, from 2006

## Fortis

Manager, steel, hand winding, AS calibre 1475, from 1954

## Dubey & Schaldenbrand

Steel, automatic, LIP calibre 5900 (base AS 5008), 24-hour indicator (second zone time), from 2006

## Fortis

B-42 Official Cosmonauts' Chrono Alarm, steel, automatic, Fortis calibre (base ETA 7750), chronograph, alarm movement with automatic winding, 24-hour indicator (second zone time), from 2006

## IWC

GST Automatic Alarm, titanium, automatic, IWC calibre C.197, from 1999

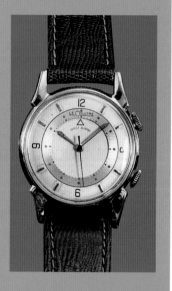

**Jaeger-LeCoultre**
LeCoultre Wrist Alarm, steel/gold-plated, hand winding, calibre JLC 814, from 1951

**Jaeger-LeCoultre**
Memovox, steel, hand winding, calibre JLC 489/1, from 1951

**Jaeger-LeCoultre**
Master Memovox, red gold, automatic, JLC 914, perpetual calendar with double moon phase display, from 2006

**Jaeger-LeCoultre**
Memovox Automatic, steel, automatic, calibre JLC 916, from 1951

*memorare* (to remember) and *vox* (voice). The first Memovox watches raised their voices by having the rapidly moving hammer strike a pin that protruded into the movement from the inner side of the case back and made a rasping sound.

Today, several generations of watch later, the Memovox produces a restrained, dulcet ring. This comes from a semicircular gong which is screwed into the back and thus uses the whole case as a resonating body. Whilst the movement is automatically wound by a rotor, the wearer has to wind the alarm movement by hand. For winding and setting the alarm, all Memovox versions use the crown at two o'clock.

## Vulcain's Crickets

The second classic among wristwatch alarms is Vulcain's Cricket. It owes its name to the scraping and chirping sound made by crickets, unpleasant to some ears. Hearers are reminded of it as soon as the Cricket rings. This wristwatch

**Junghans**
Minivox, steel, hand winding,
Junghans calibre 89, from 1960

**Jaeger-LeCoultre**
Master Grand Réveil, platinum, automatic
JLC 909/1, from 1999

**Jaeger-LeCoultre**
Master Compressor Memovox, steel,
automatic JLC 918 (base JLC 916),
bidirectional rotating bezel under glass,
compressor crown seal system, from 2006

alarm was developed in 1947 by Robert Ditisheim, former boss of the Swiss watch company, Vulcain. His greatest concern was that the alarm did not sound loud enough. His friend, a professor of physics, Paul Langevinb, made the helpful suggestion of using a little bell made of beryllium bronze to solve the problem.

'My father had been working on this problem for seven years', Robert Ditisheim's son, Michael, later said, describing these efforts. Since then, there has been a resonance space under the outer case lid, separated by a second back. The alarm hammer now strikes the anvil of this inner back and truly does make enough noise to wake you up. The double-walled case back remains a special feature of the Vulcain wristwatch alarm to this day. It is also worth mentioning the clever yet simple operation of the Cricket. The time is set quite normally by pulling out the crown, which is then pushed in again. To set the alarm movement, you press the button at two o'clock. The crown will jump out again and the alarm time can then be set. The

**Jaeger-LeCoultre**
AMVOX 1 Alarm, steel, automatic JLC 918 (base JLC 916),
result of cooperation with the sports car company Aston
Martin, from 2006

**Maurice Lacroix**
Masterpiece Réveil Globe, steel,
automatic, ML calibre 06 (base
AS 5008), bidirectional rotating
bezel under glass, from 2006

button also serves to shorten the alarm sound if required.

Apart from Vulcain, only Jaeger-LeCoultre offered one particular quality: the alarm movement built into a divers' watch. Divers can therefore receive an acoustic warning of the time to come up. The diver can also read the decompression times required off the dial. In 1961 a Swiss diving pioneer achieved a depth record, in a lake, of 222 metres (728 feet), wearing a Vulcain Cricket Nautical.

**Péquignet**
Mooréa Réveil, steel, automatic, calibre AS 5008, from 1999

**Lémania**
Wristwatch alarm, steel, automatic, Lémania calibre LWO 2980, from 1971

**Omega**
Seamaster Memomatic, steel, automatic, calibre 980, from 1971

**Nivrel**
Alarm, steel, automatic, calibre AS 5008, from 1999

### Pierce

Alarm, steel, automatic, alarm,
AS calibre 5008, from 1976

### Sinn

Der Frankfurter Finanzplatzwecker, steel,
automatic, AS calibre 5008, automatic
winding for alarm movement, 24-hour
indicator (second zone time), bidirectional
rotating bezel under glass, from 2006

### Revue Thommen

Cricket, 1997, steel, hand winding,
Revue Thommen calibre RT 80,
from 1999

### Tiffany

Classic Alarm, steel, quartz, ETA calibre
926.301, from 1999

## The ideal travelling alarm

Two complications in one watch are in fact not
all that rare, but combining an alarm with a
time zone watch is a good idea. On journeys in
particular, a wristwatch alarm is of practical
use. A model example is the Blancpain Léman
Réveil GMT. This has a movement of more than
400 individual parts, with an automatic
winding action providing power for both the
running and the alarm movements. This
watch is very easy to operate. The time and the
second zone time are set by the crown at
the two o'clock position, the alarm time by
means of a second crown at the four o'clock
position. The alarm is switched on and off
by means of a button at the eight o'clock
position. The status quo (on or off) can be seen
on the dial. The alarm function is controlled

### Auguste Reymond

Rumba Alarm, steel, automatic,
AS calibre 5008, automatic winding
for alarm movement, from 2006

233

**Vulcain**
Cricket, red gold, hand winding,
Vulcain calibre 120, from 1960

**Ulysse Nardin**
Sonata, red gold, automatic, Ulysse Nardin
calibre UN 66, alarm with precise
adjustment to the minute, 24-hour indicator
(second zone time), from 2006

**Ulysse Nardin**
San Marco Alarm, automatic, Ulysse Nardin
calibre UN 60, from 1999

**Louis Vuitton**
Tambour Réveil Automatique, steel,
automatic, LV calibre 113 (base AS calibre
5008), automatic winding of alarm
movement, 24-hour indicator (second zone
time), from 2006

**Vulcain**
Cricket Calendar, steel/gold-plated,
hand winding, Vulcain calibre 401,
from 1954

by a classic column wheel, and its hammers strike a gong such as is found in repeater watches. This watch alarm sounds just as melodious.

Ulysse Nardin has achieved a comparable effect with the Sonata. It owes its name to the melodic sound of the signal, created by a gong made of hardened steel. Screwed down at one end only, it is wound around the movement and can therefore be set into a marked oscillating motion by the alarm hammer. A special feature of the Sonata is that the alarm time can be set to the exact minute and the zone time can be effortlessly adjusted by a plus and a minus button.

**Vulcain**
Cricket Nautical, steel, hand winding, Vulcain calibre 120, with diver's decompression table on the dial, from 1961

**Vulcain**
Lady Millésime 1928, steel, hand winding, Vulcain calibre V-11, from 2006

**Vulcain**
Aviator Elapse Time, steel, hand winding, Vulcain calibre V-11, from 2006

**Vulcain**
Aviator Dual-Time, steel, hand winding, Vulcain calibre V-12, additional 12-hour indicator (second zone time), from 2006

# 7. TOURBILLON WATCHES

The basic idea of the tourbillon is as simple as it is ingenious. If a watch in a vertical position is allowed to rotate slowly but constantly around the arbour of the hands, all errors of the escapement regulator will have been corrected after each revolution. However, it is hardly practical to allow the whole watch to rotate. Breguet therefore concentrated on the regulator and devised a mechanism that ensured that the entire escapement within the movement rotated around its own arbour. The design and construction of a tourbillon are still considered the crown of watchmaking skill today – and they are correspondingly expensive.

**Audemars Piguet**

Tourbillon II, yellow gold, automatic, AP calibre 2875, power reserve indicator, from 1999

**Arnold & Son**

Tourbillon, white gold, automatic, A & S calibre 1805, from 2006

**Audemars Piguet**

Edward Piguet Tourbillon large date, white gold, hand winding, AP calibre 2874, from 2006

Clockmaking in the eighteenth century was characterized more than ever before by concerted efforts to force mechanical timepieces to the outermost limit of accuracy. For navigation at sea the exact time had become an absolutely vital factor. The hunt for a clock that kept the exact time reached its climax with the prize for solving the longitude problem offered in 1714 by the British Parliament. In 1773, after lengthy discussions, the prize of £20,000 went to the English clockmaker John Harrison (1693–1776). From that point on, large numbers of ships' chronometers were built, becoming ever better in performance. Although these timepieces were of modest sizes, compared to the other navigation instruments used on-board ship, they were quite unsuitable for use on land, being far too big and sensitive. Many clockmakers therefore found a new challenge in the optimization of travel clocks and watches.

The biggest problem for precision clockmakers lay in the various awkward qualities of the metals available at the time. It seemed impossible to solve. At different temperatures. metals change their physical qualities and their dimensional accuracy. The escapement assembly, composed of balance wheel and balance spring, was particularly badly affected. The steel spiral was sensitive to temperature changes, which changed the spiral's elasticity. Increases in temperature would make the spring's power slacken, leading to the watch becoming slow. If, on the other hand, the watch were allowed to cool, it would run faster, due to the growing elasticity of the balance spring.

## Audemars Piguet

Tourbillon III, platinum, hand winding, AP calibre 2871, from 1999

## Blancpain

Léman Tourbillon large date, red gold, automatic, Blancpain calibre 6925, from 2006

## Blancpain

Villeret Tourbillon power reserve, platinum, automatic, Blancpain calibre 25, from 2006

## Blancpain

Léman Tourbillon large date, platinum, automatic, Blancpain calibre 6925, transparent dial, from 2006

## Blancpain

Le Brassus Chronograph Fly-Back Ratrappante with tourbillon, red gold, automatic, Blancpain calibre 56F9U, from 2006

**Breguet**
Tourbillon with power reserve, yellow gold, hand winding, Breguet calibre 560T, power reserve indicator, from 1999

**Breguet**
Tourbillon with power reserve indicator, platinum, hand winding, Breguet calibre 560T, retrograde 24-hour indicator, from 2006

**Breguet**
Tourbillon, yellow gold, hand winding, Breguet calibre 558T, from 1999

**Breguet**
Tourbillon Perpetual Calendar, yellow gold, hand winding, Breguet calibre 558QPT, from 1999

**Breguet**
Grande Complication Tourbillon avec Réserve de Marche, yellow gold, automatic, Breguet calibre 587DR, from 2006

**Breguet**
Tourbillon with perpetual calendar, hand winding, Breguet calibre 558QPSQ, skeleton hand-engraved movement, from 2006

## Error compensation

While clockmakers such as John Harrison and Thomas Earnshaw attempted to correct the error on the balance spring itself, Pierre Le Roy in Paris had the idea of developing a special balance wheel that would compensate for the errors. The principle underlying the self-compensating balance wheel was already known from the construction of thermometers and is based on the fact that different metals expand at different rates when temperatures rise. If two metal strips with different expansion coefficients are inseparably linked, for instance, by being rolled together, the result is a so-called bimetallic strip, which bends of its own accord when the temperature changes, because both metals expand at different rates. The ring of a self-compensating balance wheel is, depending on

the design, broken in two or three places, and is made from a bent bimetallic strip. With a two-arm self-compensating balance, the two segments of the wheel each have one end fastened to the arm. The other end is free and can therefore follow the expansion of the metal. The outer strip of the split wheel consists of the metal with the higher expansion coefficient (generally brass); the inner, like the arms, is of steel.

When the temperature rises, the brass expands and presses the free ends of the ring inwards, thus making the balance wheel smaller. The moment of inertia of the balance wheel is lowered, and it begins to oscillate faster. However, as the elasticity constant of the balance spring lessens when warmed, and this then makes the balance wheel run more slowly, the two errors balance each other out to a

**Bvlgari**
Tourbillon, yellow gold, hand winding, Bvlgari calibre MVT 9902 TB (base GP calibre 9902), power reserve indicator at the back of the movement, from 1999

**Bvlgari**
Bvlgari Tourbillon, yellow gold, hand winding, Daniel Roth calibre R&G 052, power reserve indicator at back of movement, from 2006

**Bvlgari**
Rettangolo Tourbillon, platinum, hand winding, Claret calibre 97, 100 hours' power reserve, limited edition of 20 timepieces, from 2006

241

### Philippe Charriol

Celtic Le Tourbillon, yellow gold, hand winding, Renaud & Papi calibre, from 1999

### Chopard

L.U.C. 4T Quattro Tourbillon, red gold, hand winding, L.U.C. calibre 1.02, four spring barrels, over 200 hours' power reserve, C.O.S.C. certified chronometer, from 2006

### Chopard

L.U.C. Steel Wings Tourbillon, platinum, hand winding, L.U.C. calibre 4TB, over 200 hours' power reserve, C.O.S.C. certified chronometer, from 2006

### Chronoswiss

Régulateur à Tourbillon Squelette, white gold, hand winding, Chronoswiss calibre C.361 (base STT), cantilevered minute tourbillon, two spring barrels, from 2006

### Corum

Tourbillon Mystérieuse, yellow gold, hand winding, developed exclusively for Corum by Christopher Claret, transparent bottom plates and sapphire bridges, from 1999

certain extent. How difficult it is to correct one error by means of another, watchmakers had to discover in practice, for what looks all right in a calculation will in reality often behave quite differently from the way it was worked out on paper. To take care of the fine-tuning, self-compensating balance wheels are provided with numerous threaded holes for the attachment of various adjusting and weighting screws, which can influence, among other things, the extent of the compensation.

## Mobility creates new problems

As could have been expected, compensating for so-called temperature errors paved the way for plenty of other potential errors no one had previously thought of. The fact that the bimetallic strips that made the balance wheel rings did not behave as one would have wished was particularly annoying. After a change in temperature, they did not return to their original conditions, and also, due to a lack of precision in manufacture, they did not behave symmetrically. This meant that the centre of gravity of the entire escapement was constantly on the move and only very rarely was exactly within the axis of the balance wheel.

This was not so very important where ships' chronometers were concerned, as the balance wheel was always oscillating on a horizontal

**Roger Dubuis**
Sympathie Tourbillon, white gold, hand winding, RD calibre 1102, perpetual calendar, limited edition of 28, from 2006

**Roger Dubuis**
Golden Square Flying Tourbillon, rose gold, hand winding, RD calibre 03, crown push button to correct date, limited edition of 28, from 2006

**Gérald Genta**
Octo Tourbillon Incontro, platinum, automatic, Gérald Genta calibre 9051, retrograde hour display, quartz movement with digital display on the back of the case including alarm, chronograph, and calendar, from 2006

**De Witt**
Académia Tourbillon Différentiel, titanium/red gold, hand winding, De Witt calibre DW 8002, cantilevered minute tourbillon, 110 hours' power reserve, from 2006

plane. For pocket watches, on the other hand, obvious variations in the movement in various vertical positions were most irritatingly evident.

## Yet another new invention

On 23 December 1800 – the Republican Calendar of revolutionary France had the date Nivose 3, year IX – Breguet sent a note to the Minister of the Interior: 'I am honoured to submit to you a mémoire with a description of an invention that can be applied to timepieces, and which I would like to name "*Régulateur à Tourbillon*", and also request the privilege of being the sole individual permitted to construct such regulators for ten years'.

Breguet subsequently described his *régulateur* as being in a position 'to annul the anomalies caused by the various positions of the centre of

**Girard-Perregaux**
Tourbillon Président, yellow gold, hand winding, GP calibre 9800, minute tourbillon on the back of the movement, from 1999

**Girard-Perregaux**
Tourbillon with three gold bridges, platinum, GP calibre 9600, minute tourbillon, movement cut to skeleton form and engraved by hand, from 1999

**Girard-Perregaux**
Tourbillon ww.tc, rose gold, hand winding, GP calibre 098G0, minute tourbillon on the back of the works, 24-hour indicator (world time), from 2006

**Girard-Perregaux**
Vintage Tourbillon with three gold bridges, red gold, automatic, GP calibre 9600C, minute tourbillon, micro-rotor, from 2006

**Girard-Perregaux**
Vintage Tourbillon with gold bridge, red gold, automatic, GP calibre 9610C, minute tourbillon, micro-rotor, from 2006

gravity of the escapements'. A few months later, on 26 June 1801, or Messidor 7, year IX, Breguet received the desired patent, giving him the exclusive right for ten years to be the sole individual producing such tourbillons. The first watch with a *régulateur à tourbillon* was sold in 1805. A mere 35 such watches were sold in Breguet's lifetime.

It was typical of Breguet's sense of self-advertisement and what we would nowadays call 'marketing' that he straight away gave his invention an appropriate name. 'Tourbillon' means whirlwind, yet in the 1772 *Encyclopedia* of Diderot and d'Alembert the word is also used, in analogy to Descartes' *Principes*, to refer to the momentum that kept the planets rotating about the sun; in other words, a very even motion. Many other terms, such as 'rotational motion',

**Glashütte Original**
Julius Assmann Drehganguhr, rose gold, hand winding,
Glashütte Original calibre 51, cantilevered minute tourbillon
on back of works, perpetual calendar, from 1999

**Glashütte Original**
Alfred Hellwig Tourbillon, rose gold,
hand winding, Glashütte Original
calibre 41, cantilevered minute
tourbillon, from 1999

**Hublot**
Big Bang Tourbillon, steel,
hand winding, cantilevered
minute tourbillon, limited
edition of nine, from 2006

**Glashütte Original**
PanoMatic Tourbillon, rose gold,
automatic, Glashütte Original calibre
93, cantilevered minute tourbillon,
limited edition of 100, from 2006

have been used in an attempt to give the movement another name, but without a chance of success.

## The trick with the turn

The basic idea of the tourbillon is as simple as it is ingenious. If a pocket watch is allowed to rotate in a vertical position slowly but steadily around the arbour of the hands, all errors in the centre of gravity of the escapement would have to be corrected after each rotation. It is, of course, hardly practical to rotate the whole watch. Breguet therefore concentrated on the escapement regulator and devised a mechanism to ensure that the entire escapement assembly rotated within the movement on its own arbour.

The technical drawings show a little cage of steel, physically attached in a rotatable position to the main plate. The rotatable cage is moved by the third wheel across a pinion

**Jaeger-LeCoultre**
Master Gyrotourbillon, platinum, hand winding, JLC calibre 177, spherical tourbillon with two rotating arbours, direct display of equation of time, perpetual calendar, limited edition of 75, from 2006

**F.P. Journe**
Tourbillon Souverain à seconde morte, platinum, hand winding, escapement with seconde morte, cantilevered minute tourbillon, power reserve indicator, from 2006

**Daniel JeanRichard**
TV Screen Tourbillon, platinum, automatic, JR calibre (base Girard-Perregaux), from 2006

**A. Lange & Söhne**
Tourbillon pour le Mérité, yellow gold, hand winding, Lange calibre L.902.0, driving power regulated via chain and fusée plus stepped and planetary gear, from 1999

riveted to the arbour. It is situated, therefore, in the place where the second hand is normally to be found. For watches with anchor escapements, the balance wheel, anchor, and escapement are arranged on a little platform in the centre of the tourbillon cage, with the balance wheel generally being in the middle and turning on its own arbour. On the arbour of the escapement wheel there is a pinion, engaging through the floor of the cage with a fixed cogwheel fastened to the plate. While the third wheel sets the cage rotating, this rotation is braked once more by the escapement wheel pinion engaging with the fixed cogwheel.

The rotational movement of the cage can be set at different speeds. In modern watches, tourbillons perform a full rotation about once

### Movado

Museum Tourbillon, platinum, hand winding, minute tourbillon on the back of the movement, individual piece, from 2006

### Richard Mille

Tourbillon RM 002-V2, red gold, hand winding, RM calibre 002-V2, bottom plate made from carbon fibre, from 2006

### Franck Muller

Cintrée Curvex Tourbillon Imperiale, yellow gold, hand winding, FM calibre TFM95, from 1999

### Franck Muller

Long Island Tourbillon, white gold, hand winding, FM calibre 2001, from 2006

### Richard Mille

Tourbillon RM 009 Felipe Massa, aluminium-silicon carbide, hand winding, RM calibre 009 FM, special series to honour the Brazilian Formula 1 racing driver Felipe Massa, limited edition of 25, from 2006

### Parmigiani

Kalpa XL Tourbillon, rose gold, hand winding, Parmigiani calibre 500, 30-second tourbillon, from 2006

### Patek Philippe

10 Jours Tourbillon, platinum, hand winding, Patek Philippe calibre 28-20REC10 PS IRM, minute tourbillon on the back of the movement, ten-day power reserve, C.O.S.C. certified chronometer, from 2006

### Piaget

Emperador Tourbillon, rose gold, hand winding, Piaget calibre 600P, cantilevered minute tourbillon, from 2006

### Robergé

Andromède II Tourbillon, white gold, hand winding, base calibre Lémania 387, from 1999

### Daniel Roth

Tourbillon Double Face, yellow gold, hand winding, base calibre Lémania 2187, date and power reserve indicators on the back of the movement, from 1999

### Daniel Roth

Tourbillon 200 Hours Power Reserve, rose gold, hand winding, Daniel Roth calibre DR 720, date and power reserve indicator on the back of the movement, from 2006

a minute. This makes it possible to mount the second hand directly on the cage arbour. Breguet's first tourbillons were also minute tourbillons. He did experiment later with tourbillon cages that rotate once on their own arbour in four or even six minutes, but kept coming back to the minute tourbillon.

Breguet's tourbillon did indeed help the pocket watch to maintain even greater precision, but for him that seemed to have been more of a pleasant side effect. The essential point for him and for his reputation was the fact the he had once again devised a mechanism that could not be so quickly copied by anyone else. Tourbillon watches were bought, then as now, mainly by wealthy people who were less interested in the precise time than in the exclusive nature of this little technical gem. As a tourbillon in a watch fulfils no visible additional function that can be proudly shown off, it was not long before the first watches with pierced dials were made, allowing observers to watch the mechanism at work.

**Alain Silberstein**
Tourbillon Kronomarine, steel, hand winding, base calibre Lémania 2387, minute tourbillon, limited edition of ten, from 1999

**Alain Silberstein**
Tourbillon Emaille Dragon, yellow gold, hand winding, base calibre Lémania LWO 387, minute tourbillon, enamel dial in cloisonné technique, limited edition of ten, from 1999

**Alain Silberstein**
Tourbillon African Summer, steel, hand winding, ASC calibre 1.1 (base STT), minute tourbillon, limited edition of 500, from 2006

**Alain Silberstein**
Tourbillon Emaille Squelette, sapphire/titanium, hand winding, base calibre Lémania LWO 8701, minute tourbillon, limited edition of ten, from 1999

249

**Vacheron Constantin**
Les Complications Tourbillon,
yellow gold, hand winding,
Vacheron Constantin calibre 2250,
four spring barrels, 250 hours' power
reserve, double power reserve
indicator, from 2006

**Vacheron Constantin**
Saint-Gervais, platinum, hand
winding, Vacheron Constantin calibre
1760, two spring barrels, power
reserve indicator, from 1999

**Ulysse Nardin**
Royal Blue Tourbillon, platinum, hand winding, Ulysse Nardin
calibre UN 74, flying minute tourbillon, from 2005

**Ulysse Nardin**
Freak, white gold, hand winding, Ulysse Nardin calibre UN 01,
carousel tourbillon with patented Dual-Ulysse escapement,
parts of the movements act as hands, from 2005

**Union**
Johannes Dürrstein 3, rose
gold, hand winding, Union
calibre 45-01, flying minute
tourbillon, from 2005

## Exclusivity is the answer

It is still extremely difficult today to build a tourbillon. Apart from the fact that it is supposed to look fascinatingly delicate and filigreed, a tourbillon is, of course, mainly intended to improve the running of a watch. The complicated mechanism, however, is in exactly the place where the movement has the least power. The drive the second wheel can impart to the escapement is some 300 times weaker than on the teeth of the spring barrel. Friction in this part of the watch must therefore be as low as possible. If the whole mechanism is then supposed to rotate, it must be as light and filigreed as possible. For this reason, it is a very special challenge for a clock designer and clockmaker to construct a functioning tourbillon that also demonstrates better running values than the ordinary pendulum. It is even more difficult to miniaturize the whole thing so that it fits into a wristwatch.

**Harry Winston**
Excenter Tourbillon, platinum,
hand winding, HW calibre 400A,
from 2006

### Louis Vuitton
Tourbillon Tambour Monogram, white gold, hand winding,
third wheel can be customized as desired (e.g. as a monogram),
from 2006

### Vulcain
Tourbillon Imperial Gong, rose gold, hand winding,
Vulcan calibre V-30, cantilevered minute tourbillon,
alarm signal on two gongs, from 2006

### Zenith
Chronomaster XXT Tourbillon, rose gold, automatic,
Zenith calibre 4005 El Primero, minute tourbillon,
chronograph, 2006

**Harry Winston**
Tourbillon, platinum, hand winding,
from 2006

# 8. CALENDAR WATCHES

One of the useful additional functions of a watch, even in the electronic age, is undoubtedly indication of the date. Things are made even easier for the wearer if the watch also shows the weekday, month, and even the year. Right at the top of this category is the perpetual calendar, which even leap years cannot throw off course.

**Angelus**
Chronodato, steel/gold-plated,
hand winding, full calendar,
chronograph, from 1948

**Audemars Piguet**
Royal Oak Offshore, yellow gold,
automatic, AP calibre 2120 QP,
full calendar, from 1999

**Audemars Piguet**
Royal Oak Quantième Perpétuel,
yellow gold, automatic, AP calibre
2120 QP, perpetual calendar,
from 1999

**Audemars Piguet**
Quantième Perpétuel Jubilee Model,
red gold, automatic, AP calibre,
2120 QP, perpetual calendar,
from 1999

**Audemars Piguet**
Millenary Quantième Perpétuel, yellow
gold, automatic, AP calibre 2120 QP,
perpetual calendar, from 1999

Date indicators were among the earliest additional displays for mechanical clocks. For the standard date indicator on wristwatches, there is a train on the side of the base plate facing the dial and, depending upon the design, perhaps a few levers and a ratchet. One of the wheels of the train engages with the hour wheel, which carries the hour hand, and is driven by it. The date control system moves continuously along with the hands and changes the date, either slowly over several hours or suddenly with a jerk at midnight. This is done by a ring of fine brass plate, more rarely of plastic, placed at the outer edge of the movement plate. The ring bears the numbers 1 to 31 and has a toothed inner ring. Engaging with this ring is an attachment placed on a wheel controlled by the movement. The ratchet mentioned above serves to keep the date ring at rest after the switch-over, maintaining the current date exactly under the date window in the dial even when the watch is moved.

The basic principle has been improved upon in many ways by watch designers. The so-called quick switch, for example, moves the date on by one day at midnight exactly using a spring tightened for several hours beforehand by the movement. Watches that do not have this device switch over gradually from around 9.00 p.m. to midnight. The technical process for the fast date correction option was also improved – this is essential when a mechanical watch has not been wound for a few days.

**Blancpain**
Chronograph 2100 Perpetual Calendar, yellow gold, automatic, Blancpain calibre 5585, perpetual calendar, chronograph, from 1999

**Baume & Mercier**
Calendar Chronograph, rose gold, calibre W72, full calendar, from 1953

**Blancpain**
Moon Phase Calendar 2100, yellow gold, automatic, Blancpain calibre 1153, full calendar, from 1999

**Blancpain**
2100 Military Moon Phase Calendar, steel, automatic, Blancpain calibre 1153, full calendar, from 1999

255

## Blancpain

Chrono Fly-Back Perpetual Calendar, steel, automatic, Blancpain calibre 55F8, perpetual calendar, chronograph with Fly-Back function, from 1999

## Blancpain

Le Brassus Equation Marchante, platinum, automatic, Blancpain calibre 3863, perpetual calendar, equation of time indicator, from 2006

## Blancpain

Villeret Full Calendar with moon phase, red gold, automatic, Blancpain calibre 6763, from 2006

## Blancpain

Le Brassus Grande Complication 1735, platinum, automatic, Blancpain calibre 1735, quarter hour and minute repeater, perpetual calendar, split-second chronograph, from 2006

**Martin Braun**
Astraios, steel, automatic, ETA calibre 2892-A2 with
Martin Braun module MAB4, annual calendar, sunrise
and sunset indicator, from 2006

**Breguet**
Perpetual Linear Calendar, yellow
gold, automatic, Breguet calibre
502 QPL, perpetual calendar with
linear arranged indicators,
from 1999

**Breguet**
Perpetual Calendar Power Reserve,
yellow gold, automatic, Breguet
calibre 502 DRP, perpetual calendar
with power reserve, from 1999

The clockmaking industry performed all kinds of experiments. In one watch, the date could be pulled onwards, so to speak, by jerking the winding crown. Other mechanisms required swift pressure on the crown. Now, finally, one method has proved to be the least subject to problems. In this, the crown can be pulled out into three positions. Sitting right against the watch, the crown functions as 'winder'. When it is fully pulled out, the hands can be adjusted. Between these two positions on the winding shaft is a third, and in this one the date ring can simply be turned onwards until the correct date is displayed. Today, most watches have this particular arrangement for setting the date.

The date indicator generally leads a low-key Cinderella existence, in a small, usually four-cornered, pierced window in the dial. Often, the figures in the date indicator are so tiny that they

**Breguet**
Equation, yellow gold, automatic, Breguet calibre
502 DPE, perpetual calendar with equation of
time indicator, from 1999

are unreadable, and therefore useless, especially for elderly people with failing eyesight. The large date display was an extremely practical innovation, especially treasured, and surely not only by people of a 'reading glasses' age.

The large date display, now to be found in ever more watches, is not an invention of the 1990s, as one might assume. Individual watches with this kind of indicator were already available in the 1950s. As examples, we can here give the calibre 211, 216, and 221 of the now no longer existing Venus movement factory. In these, the date was shown by two independently turning discs.

Nowadays several watch companies offer a date indicator with a good-sized legible date. The altered hand movements and calendar mechanisms required are partly new inventions and partly based on earlier designs.

In the advertising for the lady's watch, Arkade, by A. Lange & Söhne, launched in 1994, a small watch movement was at times shown sitting inside a gigantic date ring. The figures on this date ring are about the size of the figures with which the date is shown in the Arkade's dial window. The reader of the advertisement was asked how it was possible to fit this large date indicator into such a small watch, and received the mysterious reply, 'Only Lange knows'. This sums up the very difficulty that accompanies the increase in size of the date numerals.

The solution is to replace the ring featuring the numbers 1 to 31, which encircles the movement, with two discs (or, as is the case with Lange, one disc and a cross), which are placed directly next to each other or on top of each other and are turned by the hand movement. As only the numbers 1 to 0 need to be printed, the digits can be made considerably bigger.

**Breguet**
Perpetual calendar with two spring barrels, yellow gold, automatic, Breguet calibre 591 QPT, perpetual calendar with retrograde date indicator, from 1999

**Breguet**
Perpetual Calendar, yellow gold, automatic, Breguet calibre 502 QP3, from 1999

**Breguet**
Perpetual Calendar with power reserve, yellow gold, automatic, Breguet calibre 502.3 DRP.1, from 2006

**Breguet**
Chronograph Perpetual Calendar, yellow gold, automatic, Breguet calibre 533 QP, perpetual calendar, from 1999

**Bvlgari**

Bvlgari Annual Calendar, yellow gold, automatic, Dubois-Dépraz calibre 5733 (base ETA 2892-A2), annual calendar, from 2006

**Carl F. Bucherer**

Patravi Tribute to Fritz Brun, red gold, automatic, CFB calibre 1959 (base ETA 2892-A2), perpetual calendar, chronograph, C.O.S.C. certified chronometer, from 2006

**Chopard**

Chronograph Perpetual Calendar, yellow gold, automatic, base calibre JLC 889/2, perpetual calendar, from 1999

**Chopard**

Perpetual Calendar, platinum, automatic, base calibre JLC 888, perpetual calendar, from 1999

**Chopard**

L.U.C. Lunar One, red gold, automatic, L.U.C. calibre 1.96 QP, perpetual calendar, C.O.S.C. certified chronometer, from 2006

### Chronoswiss

Lunar Full Calendar, yellow gold,
automatic, Chronoswiss calibre
C.931 (ETA 2892-A2),
from 2006

### Doxa

Chronograph with full calendar, steel,
hand winding, calibre Valjoux 72C,
from 1949

### Jaquet Droz

Quantième Perpétuel, white gold,
automatic, Jaquet Droz calibre 5863,
limited edition of 88, from 2006

### De Bethune

Perpetual Calendar with rotating moon phase, white gold,
hand winding, DB calibre 2004, moon phase designed
as sphere, from 2006

### Dubey & Schaldenbrand

Spiral VIP, rose gold, automatic, ETA calibre 7751, full calendar,
chronograph, from 2006

## More than just a date

The weekday indicator is generally moved on by the same mechanism that moves the date, but sometimes by a separate wheel. The indicator mechanism is like that of the date indicator. The weekdays only are inscribed on a thin sheet metal ring equipped with teeth, either once or in varying sequences one after the other. The designers need to take into account that Monday always follows Sunday, no matter whether we are at the end of a month of 30 days or in the February of a leap year. Occasionally there are quick switch arrangements that can be activated by pressing the crown, whereby a light pressure moves the date on, and stronger pressure the weekday indicator. It was of course in the nature of these arrangements that mistakes in switching were often made and therefore the whole month had to be repeated.

Other combinations made no provision for moving on the weekday (to correct the watch, therefore, it had to be moved on by one week) and the date change was moved forwards by pulling on the crown. In this last method, the simplest way has once again proved to be the best. Nearly all date and weekday corrections are today done by pulling the winder shaft out to the middle position mentioned above, and then by turning the crown to the left to set the date, setting the weekday by turning it to the right, or vice versa.

## Full and annual calendars

If the display of day and date is not enough for you, choose the full calendar. This term is used for watches that also indicate the month. The month indicator is controlled by the date star, a toothed wheel with 31 teeth that makes one rotation every month and then turns the month one step onwards with the month pointer positioned above it. However, as you can deduce from this explanation, the full calendar only recognizes months with 31 days. In months

**Roger Dubuis**
Sympathie bi-retrograde perpetual calendar, rose gold, automatic, RD calibre 5772, date and weekday, with retrograde indicator, from 2006

**Dubey & Schaldenbrand**
Moondate, rose gold, automatic, ETA calibre 7751, full calendar, chronograph, from 1999

**Roger Dubuis**
Golden Square Perpetual Calendar, rose gold, automatic, RD calibre 5739, from 2006

**Ebel**
Perpetual Calendar, yellow gold, automatic, Ebel calibre 136 (base Zenith 400 El Primero), perpetual calendar, chronograph, from 1999

**Eberhard**
Chronograph with full calendar,
yellow gold, hand winding, ETA calibre
7761, full calendar, chronograph,
from 1999

**Eberhard**
Replica, sterling silver, hand winding,
from 1950

**Eberhard**
Navymaster, yellow gold, hand winding, ETA calibre
7761, full calendar, chronograph, C.O.S.C. chronometer,
from 1999

**Louis Erard**
1931 Moon Phase, steel, automatic, ETA calibre 2824-2
with full calendar module by Dubois-Dépraz, from 2006

**Glashütte Original**
1845 Perpetual Calendar, yellow gold, automatic,
Glashütte Original calibre 49-01, from 1999

with 30 or fewer days the wearer needs to act
and jump over the non-existent day with an
adjustment button, thus moving on to the first
of the next month. The next stage on is the
annual calendar, which only needs correcting in
February. Four-year calendars, often also
referred to as semi-perpetual calendars, only
lose their place every leap year. The wearer only
needs to make a correction on 29 February.

## Watches for your great-grandchildren

The crème de la crème are perpetual calendars,
which will give the time, day, date, month, year,
or at least leap year, and phase of the moon for
over 100 years – until 1 March 2100, to be
specific. The year 2100, which probably few of
today's proud owners of such complicated

**Glashütte Original**
Karree Perpetual Calendar, yellow gold,
automatic, Glashütte Original calibre
42-01, from 1999

**Eterna**
Calendar watch, yellow gold, hand
winding, calibre 1118H, full calendar,
from 1945

**Girard-Perregaux**
Vintage XXL Perpetual Calendar,
rose gold, automatic, GP calibre
3170, perpetual calendar,
chronograph, from 2006

**Glashütte Original**
Senator Perpetual Calendar, rose gold,
automatic, Glashütte Original calibre
100-02, from 2006

263

**Heuer**

Chronograph, full calendar, steel, hand winding, calibre Valjoux 730, from 1950

**IWC**

Novecento, yellow gold, automatic, IWC calibre C.96061, perpetual calendar with moon phase indicator, from 1999

**IWC**

Portuguese Perpetual Calendar, red gold, automatic, IWC calibre 50611, double moon phase indicator, from 2006

**IWC**

Da Vinci Rattrapante, yellow gold, automatic, IWC calibre 79251, perpetual calendar with moon phase indicator, chronograph with split-second function, from 1999

**IWC**

Portofino, platinum, hand winding, IWC calibre C.18561, perpetual calendar with moon phase indicator, from 1999

264

## Jaeger-LeCoultre

Calendar watch, steel/gold-plated, hand winding, JLC calibre 806AW, full calendar, moon phase indicator, from 1945

## Jaeger-LeCoultre

Master Moon, steel, automatic, JLC calibre 891/448, full calendar, moon phase indicator, from 1999

watches will live to see, will, as a so-called secular year, not be a leap year. There will therefore be no 29 February in that year. In the Gregorian calendar that we all follow, this is supposed to happen every four years, but with full centuries only if these can be divided by 400. Up until that date, however, the watches on sale today will deliver the expected information. Depending, of course, on whether the spring is regularly wound up.

The 'perpetual' element has its limits – for example, a slackened spring. If, therefore, an enthusiast for these complex watches wants to wear another timepiece, perhaps for sport or when travelling – it could be a good idea, given the high value of these masterpieces – he or she would have to make sure that the perpetual calendar continues to be supplied with energy. The watch must therefore be wound by hand

## IWC

Da Vinci, red gold, automatic, IWC calibre 79261, moon phase indicator, chronograph, from 2006

## Jaeger-LeCoultre

Calendar watch, steel/yellow gold, hand winding, JLC calibre 494/1, full calendar, moon phase indicator, from 1945

**Jaeger-LeCoultre**
Master Perpetual, red gold,
automatic, JLC calibre 889/1-440/1,
perpetual calendar, moon phase
indicator, from 1999

**Jaeger-LeCoultre**
Master Calendar, red gold, automatic,
JLC calibre 924, full calendar, moon
phase and power reserve indicator,
from 2006

**Jaeger-LeCoultre**
Master Eight Days Perpetual, red
gold, automatic, JLC calibre 876,
perpetual calendar, from 2006

**JeanRichard**
TV Screen Perpetual Calendar, white
gold, automatic, JR calibre 80 33 QJ,
perpetual calendar, from 2006

**Kelek**
Grande Complication, yellow gold, automatic, Kelek calibre 2152-24S, perpetual calendar, chronograph, from 1999

**F.P. Journe**
Octa Calendar, platinum, automatic, F.P. Journe calibre 1300-2, annual calendar with retrograde date indicator, from 2006

**Kelek**
52 Calendar Weeks, steel, automatic, Kelek calibre 9252 (base ETA 2892), calendar week indicator, from 1999

**Kelek**
Semi-perpetual calendar, steel/yellow gold, automatic, Kelek calibre 5700 (base ETA 2892-A2), from 1999

every other day at the latest, or permanently turned by a watch mover, so that the automatic oscillating weight can tighten the spring. This secures the constant display of all time and calendar information, but has the disadvantage of continuous wear and tear, without allowing you to enjoy this technical wonder. Many of these marvellously complicated watches will probably in any case have to spend their existence in the dark safe of a collector, who would like to own such a watch but would not use it. It's a pity, really.

## A short aside – moon phase indicators

The moon, feminine in gender in Latin-based languages and honoured in many ancient cultures as a symbol closely connected with fertility, exercises a fascination even over people with no feel for mysticism. At times, the power of the moon is very highly esteemed, for instance, in the case of a hairdresser in Saxony,

**Kurth**
Calendar watch, rose gold, automatic, historic Longines calibre with calendar module, from 1999

267

**Maurice Lacroix**

Moon phase watch, steel, automatic, ML calibre 37 (base ETA 2824-2), full calendar, from 1999

**Maurice Lacroix**

Masterpiece Phase de Lune Tonneau, steel, automatic, ML calibre 37 (base ETA 2824-2), full calendar, from 2006

**Maurice Lacroix**

Masterpiece Lune Rétrograde, yellow gold, hand winding, ML calibre 104, (base ETA 6498-2) retrograde date indicator, 2006

**Maurice Lacroix**

Masterpiece Calendrier Rétrograde, steel, hand winding, ML calibre 76 (base ETA 6498-2), retrograde date indicator, from 2006

**A. Lange & Söhne**

Langematic Perpetual, yellow gold, automatic, Lange calibre L922.1 SAX-O-Mat, perpetual calendar, 24-hour indicator, from 2006

**Longines**
Evidenza Moon Phase, steel, automatic, Longines L600
(base ETA 2892-2), full calendar, from 2006

Germany, who cut her customers' hair at the full moon (because certain toxins are supposed to concentrate in the ends of the hairs at that time), and thereby broke the strict German laws on hours of business.

In earlier centuries, astrology was indeed generally far more involved in people's lives than it is today, and the moon awarded an importance far in excess of its scientifically proven effects on events on earth (on the tides, for example). The continual changing of the moon from slender crescent to rounded full moon and back to new moon was an early stimulus to clockmakers to demonstrate the different forms of our planet's companion, and in particular their regular pattern, by means of a display on a clock.

**Longines**
Chronograph Moon Phase, yellow gold, hand winding, calibre Valjoux 72C, full calendar, chronograph, from 1979

**Longines**
Master Collection Moon Phase, steel, automatic, Longines calibre L678 (base ETA 7751), full calendar, 24-hour indicator, from 2006

**Marcello C.**
Full calendar, steel, hand winding, ETA calibre 6497, from 1999

**Longines**
Conquest Replica Chrono Moon Phase, steel, automatic, Longines calibre L687.2 (base ETA 7751), full calendar, chronograph, 24-hour indicator, from 2006

## Minerva

Chronograph with full calendar, steel, hand winding, calibre Valjoux 723, from 1955

## Mühle Glashütte

Business-Timer, steel, automatic, ETA calibre 2892-A2 with module built on, calendar week indicator, from 2006

## Franck Muller

Cintrée Curvex Chrono Master Calendar, rose gold, automatic FM calibre 1870, full calendar, chronograph, from 1999

## Franck Muller

Cintrée Curvex Perpetual Calendar, yellow gold, automatic, FM calibre RFM93, perpetual calendar, quarter hour and minute repeater, from 1999

## H. Moser & Cie

Moser-Perpetual 1, red gold, hand winding, perpetual calendar with small month indicator cut out of the centre, from 2006

## Franck Muller

Rattrapante Q.P. Tourbillon, platinum, automatic, FM calibre 1790, perpetual calendar, chronograph with split-second function, from 1999

## Franck Muller

Long Island Master Calendar, white gold, automatic, FM 2800, full calendar, from 2006

## Franck Muller

Cintrée Curvex Chrono QP Rétrograde, yellow gold, automatic, FM calibre 5888 BR, perpetual calendar with retrograde indicators, chronograph, from 2006

## Nivrel

One year calendar, steel, automatic, ETA calibre 2892-2 with calendar module, from 1999

## Franck Muller

Cintrée Curvex Quantième Perpétuel, white gold, automatic, FM calibre 5888 BR, perpetual calendar with retrograde month indicator, from 2006

## Nivrel

Perpetual calendar 52 weeks, steel, automatic, ETA calibre 2892-2 with calendar module calendar week indicator, from 1999

**Omega**
Cosmic, red gold, hand winding, calibre 381, full calendar, from 1940

**Parmigiani**
Toric Quantième Perpetual Rétrograde, white gold, automatic, Parmigiani calibre 333, perpetual calendar with retrograde date indicator, from 2006

**Patek Philippe**
Perpetual Calendar, white gold, automatic, Patek Philippe calibre 27-4600, perpetual calendar with moon phase display, from 1963

**Oris**
Complication Tonneau, steel, automatic, Oris calibre 581 (base ETA 2688/2671) 24-hour indicator, from 1999

There are very practical reasons for this, because particularly in the temperate zones of our planet the sky is often cloudy for days on end and the Earth's satellite cannot be seen. What a good thing it is, then, to have a watch that shows the state of affairs above the clouds. Now, it may be comparatively simple to represent the phases of the moon within a lunar month (new moon, waxing moon, first quarter, full moon, waning moon, last quarter). The function of the planet Earth, throwing its shadow and for most of the time allowing only a small part of the moon to receive sunlight, is shown on a moon phase indicator by correspondingly formed cut-outs in the dial.

Indication of the moon phase is generally via a dark blue disc turned under the dial by the movement of the hands. Two large, usually golden dots printed or polished on to the disc opposite one another are shown turn and turn about in the cut-out of the dial. The 'moon disc' lying under the watch dial rotates once in 59 days, not quite two months. The reason is the

**Patek Philippe**
Annual calendar, white gold,
automatic, Patek Philippe
calibre 315/198, from 1999

**Patek Philippe**
Chronograph Perpetual Calendar,
steel, hand winding, Patek Philippe
calibre, perpetual calendar with
moon phase indicator, only two of
these watches were made in steel,
from 1942

**Patek Philippe**
Gondolo Calendario, white gold,
automatic, Patek Philippe
calibre 324 S QA LU 24H, annual
calendar with moon phase and
24-hour indicators, from 2006

**Patek Philippe**
Chronograph Rattrapante Perpetual
Calendar, yellow gold, automatic,
Patek Philippe calibre 27-70/150,
chronograph with split-second
function, from 1999

273

### Patek Philippe

Chronograph with perpetual calendar, red gold, automatic, Patek Philippe calibre CH 27-70 Q, perpetual calendar with moon phase indicator, from 2006

### Patek Philippe

Perpetual Calendar, yellow gold, automatic, Patek Philippe calibre 240 Q, perpetual calendar with 24-hour indicator, from 2006

### Patek Philippe

Sky Moon, white gold, automatic, Patek Philippe calibre 240 LU CL, moon phase, day of lunar month and map of heavens display, from 2006

**Patek Philippe**
Perpetual Calendar, yellow gold,
automatic, Patek Philippe calibre
315/136, perpetual calendar with
retrograde date indicator, from 1999

**Paul Picot**
Firshire Quantième Perpétuel, rose gold,
automatic, perpetual calendar, from 1999

**Daniel Roth**
Perpetual Calendar, rose gold, automatic,
Daniel Roth calibre, from 1999

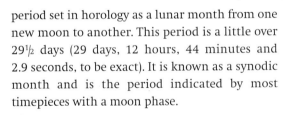

period set in horology as a lunar month from one new moon to another. This period is a little over 29½ days (29 days, 12 hours, 44 minutes and 2.9 seconds, to be exact). It is known as a synodic month and is the period indicated by most timepieces with a moon phase.

It is easy to work out that this will soon lead to considerable inaccuracies. Two synodic months are not exactly 59 days long, but 59 days, 1 hour, 28 minutes and 5.8 seconds. In high-quality watches, this circumstance is compensated for by specially calculated movements. In the Referenz 5055 by Patek Philippe, for example, the divergence between the moon phase indicator and the actual moon cycle will amount to more than one day only after 122 years and 45 days.

Lange & Söhne have developed a mechanism where a round disc under the dial turns in a period of three moon phases, about 88 days and just under 15 hours. This disc shows a section of its

**Rolex**
Perpetual Chronometer Precision, steel,
automatic, from 1950

**Robergé**
Andromède II, perpetual calendar,
yellow gold, automatic, Dubois-
Dépraz calibre 5100, from 1999

**Daniel Roth**

Instantaneous Perpetual Calendar, rose gold, automatic, Daniel Roth calibre DR 114, perpetual calendar, from 2006

**Daniel Roth**

Tourbillon Perpetual Calendar Retro Date, rose gold, automatic, Daniel Roth Calibre DR 740/M070, perpetual calendar with retrograde indicators, from 2006

**Daniel Roth**

Perpetual Calendar Moon Phases, white gold, automatic, Daniel Roth calibre DR 114, perpetual calendar, from 2006

**Schwarz Etienne**

Phase de Lune, steel, LIP calibre 3100 (base ETA 2892-2), full calendar with moon phase indicator, from 2006

**Daniel Roth**

Perpetual Calendar Time Equation, white gold, automatic, Daniel Roth calibre DR 114, perpetual calendar, length of month and time equation indicators, from 2006

### Alain Silberstein
Le Perpétuel Anniversaire, steel,
base calibre ETA 2892-A2,
perpetual calendar, from 1999

### Sothis
Osiris, steel, ETA calibre 7751,
full calendar with moon phase
indicator, chronograph, from 2006

### Sothis
Quantième Spirit of the Moon, steel,
ETA calibre 2824-2 with calendar
module, full calendar with moon
phase indicator, from 1999

### Sothis
Chronograph Spirit of the Moon,
steel, ETA calibre 7751, full calendar
with moon phase indicator,
from 1999

### Temption
Automat with complication, steel,
Temption calibre T16.2 (base ETA
2892 with calendar module) calendar
week indicator, from 1999

277

surface in the round window of the dial, and is turned forward by an extensive control movement twice a day, in almost undetectable stages. The display is so accurate that a divergence of one day will appear only after 1058 years. Assuming, of course, that the owner keeps on regularly winding the watch up until that point!

**Ulysse Nardin**
Tellurium Johannes Kepler, platinum, automatic, UN calibre 87, perpetual calendar with astronomic displays, from 1999

**Ulysse Nardin**
Perpetual Calendar Ludwig, automatic, UN calibre 33, all calendar functions can be adjusted via crown, C.O.S.C. certified chronometer, from 1999

**Union**
Tradition full calendar, steel, automatic, Union calibre 26-41, from 1999

**Union**
Johannes Dürrstein 2, rose gold, hand winding, Union calibre 40-02, perpetual calendar, from 2006

## Union

Diplomat Perpetual
Calendar, steel, automatic,
Union calibre 26-53,
perpetual calendar,
from 2006

## Universal Genève

Calendar watch with moon phase,
white gold, hand winding, calibre
291, full calendar, from 1945

## Universal Genève

Tri-Compax, yellow gold, hand
winding, calibre 281, full calendar,
chronograph, from 1948

**Universal Genève**

Complitech, steel, automatic,
Universal Genève calibre 99
(base ETA 7751), perpetual calendar,
chronograph, from 1999

**Vacheron Constantin**

Chronograph Perpetual Calendar, rose gold,
automatic, VC calibre 1136 QP, perpetual calendar,
chronograph, from 2006

**Vacheron Constantin**

Calendar watch with moon phase, red gold,
automatic, VC calibre 485, full calendar, from 2006

**Urban Jürgensen & Sønner**

Referenz 3, platinum, automatic,
perpetual calendar, from 1999

**Vacheron Constantine**

Malte Perpetual Calendar Retrograde,
platinum, automatic, VC calibre
1126 QPR, perpetual calendar with
retrograde date indicator, from 2006

**Wakmann**
Chronograph with full calendar,
hand winding, calibre Valjoux 730,
from 1975

**Vacheron Constantin**
Malte Chronograph Perpetual Calendar
Retrograde, yellow gold, automatic,
VC calibre 1126 QPR, perpetual calendar,
chronograph, from 2006

**Zenith**
Chronomaster Chronograph, yellow
gold, automatic, Zenith calibre 410
El Primero, full calendar, from 1999

**George J. von Burg**
Perpetual Calendar, rose gold, automatic,
Dubois-Dépraz calibre 2110 (base ETA
2892-A2), perpetual calendar,
chronograph, from 2006

**Xemex**
Piccadilly Calendario Reserve, rose
gold, automatic, Soprod calibre 9075
(base ETA 2892-A2) calendar week
indicator, from 2006

# 9. REPEATER WATCHES

If you want to know the time at night, you turn the light on to see your watch by. It's easy enough, these days. But in the seventeenth century, the situation was quite different. For this reason, ingenious clockmakers devised a striking mechanism for pocket watches that would inform you of the time even in darkness. Today, making repeater watches is one of the most difficult challenges a watchmaker can be set. For this reason, they are rare – and the price to be paid for them correspondingly high.

**Audemars Piguet**

Grande Complication, platinum, hand winding, AP calibre 2885, hour, quarter hour, and minute repeater, perpetual calendar, split-second chronometer, from 1999

**Audemars Piguet**

Triple Complication, yellow gold, hand winding, AP calibre 2880, hour, quarter hour, and minute repeater, perpetual calendar, chronograph, from 1999

**Audemars Piguet**

Jules Audemars tourbillon minute repeater, red gold, hand winding, AP calibre 2874, from 2006

**Audemars Piguet**

Grande Sonnerie, yellow gold, hand winding, AP calibre 2868, hour and quarter hour repetition, grand and small strike repeater movement, chronograph, from 1999

The first striking clocks were made very shortly after the first mechanical ones. This addition was introduced on very practical grounds. Clockmakers were simply concerned to broadcast time information from church towers – in those days, the only places clocks were to be found – even during the long periods of darkness in the European winter. So even during the night, those living in the parish would know at least more or less that 'the hour had struck'. At first, only full hours struck; later, there were striking movements that marked the half and quarter hours.

## Audemars Piguet

Minute Repeater Jump Hour, yellow gold, hand winding, AP calibre 2865, hour, quarter hour and minute repeater, digital jump hour indicator, from 1999

## Audemars Piguet

Jules Audemars Dynamographe, white gold, hand winding, AP calibre 2981, strike movement with 3 gongs, from 2006

## Blancpain

Le Brassus Grande Complication 1735, platinum, automatic, Blancpain calibre 1735, quarter hour and minute repeater, perpetual calendar, split-second chronograph, from 1999

## Blancpain

Minute Repeater 2100, yellow gold, automatic, Blancpain calibre 35, quarter hour and minute repeater, from 1999

285

**Blancpain**
Minute repeater, platinum, automatic, Blancpain calibre 35, quarter hour and minute repeater, from 2006

The first pocket watches with strike date from the seventeenth century. The horological genius, Abraham Louis Breguet, is given credit for the greatest share of the development of this complication, as he replaced the bells with space-saving gongs.

The practical reason alongside the above-mentioned horological challenge remained the same. Wealthy gentlemen, who in those days were the only people who could afford such watches, were to have the opportunity to tell the time even in the dark. This was the purpose of the so-called repeater clocks and watches, where a sliding bolt or push-button wound up the spring of the strike movement, which then instantly gave the time by sound, and was more or less accurate according to design.

**De Witt**
Académia Répétition Minutes, red gold, hand winding, De Witt calibre, 1188 (base Claret 88), quarter hour and minute repeater, from 2006

**Breguet**
Minute repeater, perpetual calendar, platinum, hand winding, Breguet calibre 567 RMP, from 2006

**Bvlgari**
Anfiteatro Répétition Minutes, platinum, hand winding, GP calibre 9950, quarter hour and minute repeater, from 2006

## Corum

Admiral's Cup, quarter hour repeater,
yellow gold, automatic, Corum calibre 58
(base calibre Fréderic Piguet 70), repeater
with movable images in three dial windows,
from 1999

## Roger Dubuis

MuchMore minute repeater, white
gold, hand winding, RD calibre 26,
quarter hour and minute repeater,
limited edition of 28, from 2006

## Epos

Répétition 5 Minutes, steel,
automatic, Dubois-Dépraz calibre
D 88, five minute repeater,
from 2006

## Chronoswiss

Répétition à Quarts, steel, automatic,
Chronoswiss calibre C.126 (base Enicar 165
with strike movement module), quarter hour
repeater, from 2006

The strike varied from hour strike, to hour and quarter hour strike, to timepieces with minute repeaters, where first the hours, then the quarter hours elapsed since the last full hour, and finally the minutes that had passed since the last quarter, were struck. To differentiate the strikes, different tones were created by hammers striking on two gongs, alone or in a duet. The most usual sequence is this: the deep note only sounds for the hour, the quarter hour is indicated by simultaneous stroke on both gongs, and the higher gong only is used for the minutes.

**Girard-Perregaux**
Richeville Minute Repeater, yellow gold, hand winding, GP calibre 9896, hour, quarter hour, and minute repeater, perpetual calendar, from 1999

**IWC**
Il Destriero Scafusia, red gold, hand winding, IWC calibre C.18680, hour, quarter hour, and minute repeater, tourbillon, perpetual calendar, split-second chronograph, from 1999

**Gérald Genta**
Grande Sonnerie, white gold, automatic, calibre GG 8561, hour, quarter hour, and minute repeater, grand and lesser strike movement, tourbillon, from 1999

**De Grisogono**
Occhio, red gold, hand winding, minute repeater with three gongs, dial segment mechanism opens when repeater strike is operated, from 2006

**Gérald Genta**
Octo Minute Repeater, red gold, automatic, calibre GG 8561, quarter hour and minute repeater, digital jump hour indicator, from 2006

## IWC

Grande Complication, platinum, automatic,
IWC calibre C.79091, hour, quarter hour,
and minute repeater, perpetual calendar,
chronograph, from 1999

### Kelek

Five minute repeater, yellow gold,
automatic, Kelek calibre DK 87
(base ETA calibre with module),
from 1999

### Kelek

Quarter hour repeater, steel,
automatic, Kelek calibre DK 94
(base ETA calibre with module),
from 1999

### Jaeger-LeCoultre

Minute Repeater Antoine LeCoultre, platinum,
hand winding, JLC calibre 947, power reserve
and torque indicators, from 2006

An even more complicated strike movement, the sonnerie (from the French sonner, meaning to sound, to ring) has the strikes initiated independently by the watch movement itself. A *petite sonnerie* sounds automatically when the full hour is reached, a *grande sonnerie* every quarter hour. And, of course, the strike can be activated at any time by the repeater bolt. Such a strike movement can be further extended by having extra gongs built in. You can then have a little melody played, such as the chime of 'Big Ben'. This is known as a 'carillon' – translated, that simply means a ring of bells.

**Franck Muller**
Cintrée Curvex Tourbillon Repeater, FM calibre TFM 95, hour, quarter hour, and minute repeater, tourbillon, from 1999

**Parmigiani**
Toric Corrector, platinum, hand winding, Parmigiani calibre 255, minute repeater, perpetual calendar, from 2006

**JeanRichard**
TV Screen minute repeater, white gold, hand winding, JR calibre 88 (base Claret 88), quarter hour and minute repeater, from 2006

**Franck Muller**
Conquistador, platinum, automatic, FM calibre RMQPR, hour, quarter hour, and minute repeater, perpetual calendar, from 1999

**Nivrel**
Five minute repeater, steel, automatic, Dubous-Dépraz calibre 87 (base ETA 2892-A2), from 2006

## Parmigiani

Toric Westminster, platinum, hand winding, Parmigiani calibre 252, quarter hour and minute repeater with four gongs (Westminster chimes), 24-hour indicator (second zone time), from 2006

## Daniel Roth

Grande Sonnerie, white gold, automatic, calibre DR 760 (base GG 3100), quarter hour and minute repeater with four gongs (Westminster chimes), from 2006

## Parmigiani

Kalpa XL Répétition Minutes, platinum, hand winding, Parmigiani calibre 350, quarter hour and minute repeater, from 2006

## Robergé

Andromède II Répétition Minutes, white gold, hand winding, base calibre Lémania 2179, from 1999

## Paul Picot

Atelier 818 minute repeater, rose gold, hand winding, hour, quarter hour, and minute repeater, from 1999

Today's miniaturization of the striking movement to wristwatch size is, along with the tourbillon, the crowning pinnacle of the watchmaker's art. Here, we can give only a brief indication of the complex way in which a small timepiece striking mechanism functions: the number of strikes is determined by notched cams, so-called snails, constantly rotated by the movement of the watch. Curved toothed racks are forced by the pressure of small springs to drop into the notches, at different heights according to the time, and are then transported, tooth by tooth, to their rest position by a train. The number of revolutions required in this process determines how often the hammer strikes the gong, which is wound around the watch movement.

**Daniel Roth**

Minute repeater and perpetual calendar, white gold, hand winding, Daniel Roth calibre, hour, quarter hour, and minute repeater, from 1995

**Urban Jürgensen & Sønner**

Minute repeater, platinum, hand winding, hour, quarter hour, and minute repeater, from 2006

**Daniel Roth**

Elipsocurvex Minute Repeater, white gold, automatic, calibre DR 750, minute repeater, from 2006

293

The chime is initiated, as mentioned above, by a sliding bolt. This is usually situated on the left side of the case. If it is pulled downwards, the wearer thus provides energy to the strike movement, and when it is released the chime is heard as described above. If the bolt is not moved energetically enough, the watch will sound the wrong time. For this reason, good strike movements have the so-called 'all or nothing' switch. If the repeater mechanism is activated wrongly or not firmly enough, nothing happens. However, if the watch chimes, the wearer can be sure that the number of rings corresponds to the time indicated on the dial.

**Ulysse Nardin**
San Marco Sonnerie en passant, platinum, automatic, UN calibre 75, hour and half hour repeater en passant or on request, figure on the dial moves during course of repeater chime, from 1999

**Vacheron Constantin**
Les Complications minute repeater skeleton, rose gold, hand winding, Vacheron Constantin calibre 1755 QP, hour, quarter hour, and minute repeater, perpetual calendar, from 1999

**Harry Winston**
Perpetual Calendar with minute repeater, platinum, hand winding, from 1999

**Vacheron Constantin**
Les Complications minute repeater skeleton, rose gold, Vacheron Constantin calibre 1755 QP, hour, quarter hour, and minute repeater, from 1999

## Vacheron Constantin

Tour de l'Ile, rose gold, hand winding, Vacheron Constantin calibre
2750, 16 complications, including minute tourbillon, minute
repeater, perpetual calendar, and equation of time indicator,
jubilee edition to celebrate 250th anniversary of the company,
limited edition of seven, from 2005

# 10. INDEX